how2become

PERSONALITY TESTS

www.How2Become.com

Get more career resources for passing any type of test or interview at:

www.how2become.com

Orders: Please contact How2become Ltd, Suite 3, 50 Churchill Square Business Centre, Kings Hill, Kent ME19 4YU. You can also order via the email address: info@how2become.co.uk.

ISBN: 978-1910202876

First published in 2014 by How2Become Ltd

Typeset for How2become Ltd by Anton Pshinka.

Printed in Great Britain for How2become Ltd by:
CMP (uk) Limited, Poole, Dorset.

CONTENTS

As part of this product you have also received FREE access to online tests that will help you to pass job-related assessments.

To gain access, simply go to:

www.PsychometricTestsOnline.co.uk

INTRODUCTION

Personality Tests are being used more and more in the job selection process. It allows employers to not only assess a person's suitability for the job role through their experience and skills, but also takes into consideration how a person's characteristics and personality traits could possibly help or influence the job role in some way. While it's clear that the job application process proves difficult for everyone involved, it is the first step of making an impression, so portraying yourself in the right way is important.

Personality has become increasingly resourceful over the years to identify the right person for the right job; by taking a simple test, employers are able to narrow down their choices based on performance and personality traits that are desired. Personality traits represent different tendencies and preferences rather than exact predictors of behaviour. These tests are designed to assess your individual and interpersonal behaviour and therefore gain an understanding of the type of job role that is suitable to you. Personality tests seek to establish a deeper understanding of personal characteristics that often supply employers with an insight into recognising a strong candidate. These tests provide valuable information for employers, for which they can piece together to gain an overall impression of that applicant. They are designed to reveal aspects of a person's character that employers often miss during the interview stage.

Employers will most likely use one of four main personality tests to test a person's characteristics. However, all tests are designed in a similar manner, either addressing to or at least influenced by what is known as 'the Big 5 model of personality'. The Big 5 model of personality is widely associated with psychological studies that explores the dimensions of a person's personality. It subsequently argues that every human can be understood and analysed by 5 main personality traits: **neuroticism, agreeableness, openness, extraversion and conscientiousness.** This is often referred to as the NEO-PI test.

The NEO-PI test uses these 5 main traits which are then broken down into sub-categories identifying 6 key characteristics. The 5 domains and the 30 facets facilitates a comprehensive and detailed understanding of how your personality can be broken down and understood. This book will give you the opportunity to go through and answer loads of sample questions that will then be analysed to give an informed result of your overall personality.

There are several criteria which need to be taken into consideration in order to evaluate a person's personality; the test is expected to demonstrate validity and reliability and provide a basic framework to determine a person's characteristics.

Keep in mind, that while these tests generate an overview of your personality traits, it cannot be used as definite. These questions are typical questions designed to show you how a real personality test may look. Your responses to the questions will demonstrate certain characteristics, some of which you may not agree with, and so you need to carefully consider each question and answer the question with honesty to gain a more accurate result. The test will help you engage with the types of questions you may be faced with in the real personality test and how these tests work in terms of the types of questions, analysis and interpreting the results.

Although it is often acknowledged that there are no wrong or right answers for personality tests, this book aims to provide you with the resources to gain an understanding of what you'll have to face if ever asked to take a personality test. When you undertake a real personality test it is important to remember that the test you are taking is being used as a type of screening purpose to determine the best candidate for the job. Therefore by understanding the specific characteristics that are important for your position, you will be able to fully prepare yourself. This is why it is important to go through the book carefully and gain a strong understanding of each characteristic and the meaning behind them.

Understanding the Big 5 model of personality is a vital element of the selection process and will increase your chances of success on the personality aspect of the job role.

The NEO-PI measures 30 characteristics within the Big 5 model of personality:

Neuroticism	**Agreeableness**	**Extroversion**
1. Anxiety	1. Trust	1. Warmth
2. Vulnerability	2. Straightforwardness	2. Gregariousness
3. Hostility	3. Modesty	3. Assertiveness
4. Depression	4. Compliance	4. Excitement Seeking
5. Self-Consciousness	5. Altruism	5. Positive Emotions
6. Impulsiveness	6. Tender-Mindedness	6. Activity

Conscientiousness	Openness
1. Competence	1. Fantasy
2. Order	2. Aesthetics
3. Dutifulness	3. Feelings
4. Self-Discipline	4. Actions
5. Deliberation	5. Ideas
6. Achievement Striving	6. Values

In the book, it will focus on the most up to date version of the personality test – the NEO-PI test. However, while there are other tests that could be used in your personality test, this book seeks to demonstrate an overview of the types of questions that could be found in any of the personality tests. Although the questions are specifically designed for the NEO-PI test, it will give you some indication of how other personality tests work.

In chapters 1 to 5, each chapter will refer to one of the Big 5 models – **neuroticism, agreeableness, extroversion, conscientiousness and openness.** Each of which, will provide a series of questions and/or statements to which you will be asked to rate yourself. Your answer will usually be in the form of true or false, however some questions will ask you to rate whether you 'strongly agree' or 'strongly disagree'. For example:

If I get excess change in a store, I always return it. True or false?

However, note that some of the questions are 'reversed'. This means that if you answered true, you would mark it as false when it comes to adding up your scores. For example:

It's easy for me to just kick back and relax. (Reversed) True or false?

So, if you answer true, on the score sheet provided, you must circle false in order to provide an accurate account of your results. If you answered true, your result will be a low score and because the other questions are low scores if you answered true, it means you have to reverse your answer. Vice versa, if you answered false, then you would actually circle true on the score sheet. Neutral answers remain the same.

You will then score yourself on the scoring system provided at the end of each chapter. You'll either score "high" "average" or "low", for which you will be given an explanation for each, detailing what this means in terms of personality.

Remember to consider all of your scores. If you tally up a mixture of high, average and low scores then you should take this into consideration when determining your personality.

Also in the book, in each of the chapters you will be able to work out your overall scores in each trait which allows you to look more closely at each trait, and gain a more in-depth understanding into what it all means and what this says to employers about your personality.

In chapter 6, you can also use your answers and personality traits to match up specific job role specifications and understand what traits go together. You can recognise how personality tests assist substantially in the selection process by identifying key attributes and therefore plays a vital element in stepping into any chosen career path.

CHAPTER 1 - The Big 5:

Neuroticism

CHAPTER 1 - THE BIG 5: NEUROTICISM

One of the main areas that is analysed in terms of personality is this idea of neurotic behaviour. In Psychology, it often explores neuroticism as a fundamental personality trait, which is characterised by the negative feelings and emotions of people and how they tend to cope. It identifies individuals who are prone to psychological distress and discomfort, social exclusion and emotional turmoil. In order to evaluate neuroticism, the test will focus on the feelings of apprehension, vulnerability and emotional management and the extent to which a person can manage his or her feelings.

Such tendencies of experiencing emotions such as anger, depression, anxiety and vulnerability are signs of neurotic behaviour. Neuroticism tends to assess the degree of emotional stability and impulse control which employers look out for. Obviously, a high neurotic level suggests sensitivity, vulnerability and emotionalism, whereas a low neurotic level demonstrates emotional security, control and stability.

Employers seek a low neurotic score for a workplace in order to maintain a stable and adjusted working environment. Whilst being emotionally stable is an advantage, you don't want to come across as unresponsive or 'machinelike'. In some circumstances, it is acceptable to show some level of emotion if a situation requires. However, maintaining a knowledge of when to keep your feelings bottled-up and knowing when to be responsive is crucial for any workplace.

There are 6 sub-traits that personality tests look at to measure neuroticism. These indicate emotional states of mind which are often analysed in terms of **anxiety, angry hostility, depression, self-consciousness, impulsiveness and vulnerability.**

In this chapter, it will focus on each one of these terms and assess your personality to determine your level of neurotic behaviour.

ANXIETY

One of the traits of Neuroticism is the feeling of anxiety. Anxiety is a general term that often runs parallel to traits such as fear, apprehension and worrying. People often experience a state of anxiety before stressful situations. For example, many people feel anxious before taking a test, an exam, an interview etc.

Anxiety is a term generally used to display negative emotions. These emotions affect how we act and behave and sometimes can manifest into more physical problems.

While the feeling of anxiety is quite normal and happens to everyone, it can be considered as a problem, particularly in a workplace. Showing a little anxiety in a workplace shows levels of emotional security and resilience, whereas too much anxiety signifies sensitivity and vulnerability.

These 30 questions will measure your level of anxiety and help to determine your level of neuroticism. The questions are simple; circle true or false to the statements provided and then use your answers to check your score.

**Note: Reversed means that answering 'true' to the question will result in a low score of that trait.**

1. After a meeting, I mull things over.

    | True | False |

2. I worry before important meetings.

    | True | False |

3. It's easy for me to just kick back and relax. (Reversed)

    | True | False |

4. I tend to focus on upsetting situations or events happening in my life.

    | True | False |

5. I feel fearful for no reason a lot of the time.

    | True | False |

6. I am easily alarmed, frightened or surprised.

    | True | False |

7. I am easily irritated.

True	False

8. I often feel futile.

True	False

9. I think a lot about why I do the things I do.

True	False

10. I am afraid of what awaits me in the future.

True	False

11. I have trouble falling asleep.

True	False

12. I can think about a problem for hours and still not feel that the issue is resolved.

True	False

13. I feel tense or on edge a lot.

True	False

14. I feel good about myself and the things I have accomplished. (Reversed)

True	False

15. Sometimes, I feel I am losing control.

True	False

16. I get nervous talking to people I don't know.

True	False

17. I get easily upset.

True	False

18. I remain calm in a stressful situation.

True	False

19. I feel uneasy in heated discussions.

True	False

20. I tend to take things personally.

| True | False |

21. If I sense people don't like me, I feel very uncomfortable.

| True | False |

22. Even after making a decision, I usually keep wondering if I made the right choice.

| True | False |

23. Occasionally, I have a bad mood.

| True | False |

24. I feel blue a lot of the time.

| True | False |

25. I have trouble relaxing.

| True | False |

26. I often find myself feeling lonely.

| True | False |

27. I get nervous in unfamiliar settings.

| True | False |

28. I find it hard to trust people.

| True | False |

29. I feel distant from the people around me.

| True | False |

30. I'm not happy with how my life is going.

| True | False |

Scoring System:

Circle the letter that represents your chosen answer:

Note: make sure you circle the opposite answer from your above answer for the Reversed answers

1.	T / F	2.	T / F	3. (R)	T / F	4.	T / F	5.	T / F
6.	T / F	7.	T / F	8.	T / F	9.	T / F	10.	T / F
11.	T / F	12.	T / F	13.	T / F	14. (R)	T / F	15.	T / F
16.	T / F	17.	T / F	18.	T / F	19.	T / F	20.	T / F
21.	T / F	22.	T / F	23.	T / F	24.	T / F	25.	T / F
26.	T / F	27.	T / F	28.	T / F	29.	T / F	30.	T / F

SCORE TOTAL:	True =	....	HIGH
SCORE TOTAL:	False =	....	LOW

Understanding Your Scores:

Your results on the Anxiety test will help determine your overall outcome for the trait of Neuroticism. Once you've added up how many questions you answered true to, and how many questions you answered false, it will be a clear way of distinguishing if your score was high, average or low.

If you answered true to most of the questions, then below is a detailed explanation of what this means. If you answered false to most questions, then read the description for what a low response means. An average score considers both low and high traits, so therefore you should read that description.

HIGH (mostly true)	Having a high score for anxiety indicates that you are often apprehensive, fearful, restless and nervous. You tend to fear the worse, and often suspect the worst case scenarios. You are considered pessimistic and find it difficult to show positivity. You may be afraid of specific situations or generally feel fearful. You feel tense, jittery, on edge. Although anxiety and apprehension is a natural emotional response in given situations, most employers will not hire a candidate if they are deemed too apprehensive. High anxiety levels indicate difficulty to handle pressure. Displaying high levels of anxiety causes great concern for most employers. Anxiety often leads to restlessness and vulnerability which are both signs of weakness and apprehension. The need to effectively manage workplace anxiety is imperative. Whilst at work, you need to show levels of resilience, clarity and emotional stability. Make sure you know when to show emotion and when to hold back. Not every situation requires an emotional response.
AVERAGE	An average score means that you are borderline high and low in regards to anxiousness. Whilst you may experience some levels of anxiety, you are able to demonstrate great levels of control and rationale. You sometimes experience anxiety and feel on edge, but overall you tend to show a calm and fearless approach towards your work. You are a calm and collected person, but sometimes the nerves get the better of you. Employers like to be able to see that although you may get anxious, you are able to show reticence and composure. Employers like to see a fine balance between being emotionally stable, and still being able to show passion and enthusiasm at particular moments.

LOW (mostly false)	A low score for anxiety means that you are able to deal with pressure and maintain a solid work ethic in stressful situations. You are generally considered a calm and fearless person. Having a low score for anxiety levels is more beneficial for a workplace. It illustrates your ability to be able to maintain your emotions and represent emotional security and resilience. You are often confident and optimistic. However, whilst a low anxiety level is a positive, you do not want to come across as stiff and robotic. Sometimes a situation requires some level of emotion at work in order to demonstrate your passion, enthusiasm and interest. However, knowing when to give a response and when to hold back is imperative, so make sure you pay attention to what is going on around you.

VULNERABILITY

Another trait that indicates neuroticism is vulnerability, referring to the inability to tolerate the effects of a hostile environment. Vulnerability means a person is easily offended, they feel uncomfortable in social situations and often feel like an 'outsider' to the people around them.

People who score highly on vulnerability do not take criticism well, as a matter of fact, they are more likely to take criticism, even constructed criticism, personally and therefore display a weak character. People who score low on this test shows the ability to handle criticism and indicate a person that is not afraid of difficult situations and maintain good levels of stability and composure.

For this test, you want to avoid scoring extremely high or extremely low. You do not want to come across as 'weak' or inferior to the others around you, however you also don't want to come across as 'thick-skinned' who doesn't take criticism seriously. You need to maintain an understanding of how to act in a particular situation, you want your personality to come through as resilient yet obedient, confident yet courteous.

These 30 questions will measure your level of vulnerability and will help to determine your level of neuroticism. The questions are simple; circle true or false to the statements provided and then use your answers to check your score.

Note: Reversed means that answering 'true' to the question will result in a low score of that trait.

1. If I sense people don't like me, I sometimes feel offended.

   | True | False |

2. When I am criticised, I avoid taking it personally. (Reversed)

   | True | False |

3. When I'm teased, I take it in my stride. (Reversed)

   | True | False |

4. I have a tendency to take things personally.

   | True | False |

5. People are generally too touchy and emotional.

   | True | False |

6. I get easily offended.

| True | False |

7. What others think of me is no concern of mine. (Reversed)

| True | False |

8. If I sense someone doesn't like me, I feel uneasy.

| True | False |

9. Not every friendly person is truly so; they may talk behind my back.

| True | False |

10. When people are overly nice to me, I often question their behaviour.

| True | False |

11. Sometimes I think people are gossiping about me.

| True | False |

12. I am a confident person most of the time. (Reversed)

| True | False |

13. I find heated discussions uncomfortable.

| True | False |

14. When I am publicly criticised, I don't usually feel offended. (Reversed)

| True | False |

15. I find it difficult to put my trust in someone.

| True | False |

16. In social situations, I tend to lead the group. (Reversed)

| True | False |

17. I usually back down in arguments.

| True | False |

18. I don't mind getting my point across even if it means disputing with everyone else. (Reversed)

| True | False |

19. I don't like confrontations.

| True | False |

20. I find it difficult to put my views across.

| True | False |

21. I feel under pressure a lot of the time.

| True | False |

22. I find it difficult to fit in within new environments.

| True | False |

23. I feel uncomfortable under time constraints.

| True | False |

24. I feel anxious when people confront me.

| True | False |

25. I often feel nervous.

| True | False |

26. I can't help but take things personally.

| True | False |

27. I do not mind if others don't like me. (Reversed)

| True | False |

28. I try not to let things overwhelm me.

| True | False |

29. I consider myself an anxious person.

| True | False |

30. I get annoyed easily.

| True | False |

Scoring System:

Circle the letter that represents your chosen answer:

Note: make sure you circle the opposite answer from your above answer for the Reversed answers

1. T / F	2. T / F (R)	3. T / F (R)	4. T / F	5. T / F
6. T / F	7. T / F (R)	8. T / F	9. T / F	10. T / F
11. T / F	12. T / F (R)	13. T / F	14. T / F (R)	15. T / F
16. T / F (R)	17. T / F	18. T / F (R)	19. T / F	20. T / F
21. T / F	22. T / F	23. T / F	24. T / F	25. T / F
26. T / F	27. T / F (R)	28. T / F	29. T / F	30. T / F

SCORE TOTAL:	True =	....	HIGH
SCORE TOTAL:	False =	....	LOW

Understanding Your Scores:

Your results on the Vulnerability test will help determine your overall outcome for the trait of Neuroticism. Once you've added up how many questions you answered true to, and how many questions you answered false, it will be a clear way of distinguishing if your score was high, average or low.

If you answered true to most of the questions, then below is a detailed explanation of what this means. If you answered false to most questions, then read the description for what a low response means. An average score considers both low and high traits, so therefore you should read that description.

HIGH (mostly true)	If you have answered mostly true to these Vulnerability questions, this suggests you're a person who is often cautious, take criticism poorly and feel uncomfortable in certain social situations. Employers find this trait least desirable as they want to be assured of employees who are able to take criticism effectively and be assured of confident and composed people. Vulnerability is a key element for distinguishing between strong and weak candidates. Although you do not want to come across as vulnerable, you want to come across as someone who is passionate and cares about their job role. If a person were to show no vulnerability, this suggests a lack of enthusiasm. So, ideally you want to score in between extremely high or extremely low in order to maintain a personality that shows not only stability and composure but also compassion and enthusiasm.
AVERAGE	An average score on Vulnerability means that you show both positive and negative emotions regarding a vulnerable state of mind. You are often capable of maintaining your feelings and demonstrate moderate levels of experience, maturity and composure within the working environment. However, sometimes you let your emotions take over. Whilst you may present a calm and solid exterior, sometimes you find it difficult to show your confidence, enthusiasm and passion because you feel inferior to those around you. Borderline both high and low scores means that you can show both a calm exterior and confidence, but also show naivety and overwhelming emotions. Showing that you are not completely vulnerable means that employers are more likely to feel comfortable with employing you.

LOW (mostly false)	Scoring a low score for Vulnerability has both its advantages and disadvantages. For employers, they like to see employees who are capable of maintaining their feelings and emotions and demonstrate a high level of maturity and composure within the workplace. However, if a person were to show no vulnerability, this could suggest that they show lack of enthusiasm and interest concerning criticism, deadlines and authority. Again, you want to ideally be in a position that you can show some levels of vulnerability in terms of passion and interest. However, not so much that your persona comes across as weak, uncomfortable and easily overwhelmed. For this test, you do not want to give the impression that you are easily insulted and take criticism personally, you want to come across as a person who can demonstrate high levels of strong-mindedness, assertiveness and not take criticism personally, and simply learn from previous experiences.

HOSTILITY

Neuroticism often displays levels of **hostility**. This shows a tendency to experience anger and other related states of minds such as frustration and bitterness. People with high levels of angry hostility often feel enraged, resentful and annoyed. They are people who tend to get angry when something don't go their way; they get resentful when they feel as though they've been cheated.

People with low levels of hostility show little aggression or annoyance. They get on with tasks in a calm and composed manner and do not take things personally. These people tend to show characteristics of rationale and capabilities of handling their emotions.

These 30 questions will measure your level of hostility and help to determine your level of neuroticism. The questions are simple; circle true or false to the statements provided and then use your answers to check your score.

**Note: Reversed means that answering 'true' to the question will result in a high score of that trait.**

1. I rarely act upon impulse.

True	False

2. I always keep my feelings to myself.

True	False

3. I rarely get annoyed easily.

True	False

4. People who are dominant in conversation makes me feel annoyed.

True	False

5. I rarely get frustrated with difficult people.

True	False

6. I find it difficult to keep my emotions to myself. (Reversed)

True	False

7. Sometimes I feel like cursing. (Reversed)

True	False

8. I often say offensive things to people. (Reversed)

True	False

9. Sometimes I feel like getting back at someone who hurt me. (Reversed)

True	False

10. I hardly ever get into disputes.

True	False

11. I sometimes want to be on my own as opposed to being with others.

True	False

12. I rarely feel hostile.

True	False

13. I find it difficult to restrain my emotions. (Reversed)

True	False

14. Seldom, I feel compulsive.

True	False

15. It is not often that I come into work feeling angry.

True	False

16. I often have a bad mood. (Reversed)

True	False

17. I take pressure well.

True	False

18. I avoid heated debates.

True	False

19. I avoid aggressive people.

True	False

20. I don't like aggressive behaviour.

True	False

21. I don't tolerate unacceptable and angry behaviour.

True	False

22. I usually wake up in the morning feeling calm.

True	False

23. Angry behaviour plays on my mind, I don't agree with it.

True	False

24. I often get annoyed with people who get things wrong. (Reversed)

True	False

25. I always curse other people. (Reversed)

True	False

26. Hostility is not necessary.

True	False

27. I get angry because I want to put my views across. (Reversed)

True	False

28. I seldom let my feelings affect my work.

True	False

29. I rarely have a bad mood.

True	False

30. I consider myself a friendly and polite person.

True	False

Scoring System:

Circle the letter that represents your chosen answer:

Note: make sure you circle the opposite answer from your above answer for the Reversed answers

1. T / F	**2.** T / F	**3.** T / F	**4.** T / F	**5.** T / F
6. T / F (R)	**7.** T / F (R)	**8.** T / F (R)	**9.** T / F (R)	**10.** T / F
11. T / F	**12.** T / F	**13.** T / F (R)	**14.** T / F	**15.** T / F
16. T / F (R)	**17.** T / F	**18.** T / F	**19.** T / F	**20.** T / F
21. T / F	**22.** T / F	**23.** T / F	**24.** T / F (R)	**25.** T / F (R)
26. T / F	**27.** T / F (R)	**28.** T / F	**29.** T / F	**30.** T / F

SCORE TOTAL:	True =	....	LOW
SCORE TOTAL:	False =	....	HIGH

Understanding Your Scores:

Your results on the Hostility test will help determine your overall outcome for the trait of Neuroticism. Once you've added up how many questions you answered true to, and how many questions you answered false, it will be a clear way of distinguishing if your score was high, average or low.

If you answered true to most of the questions, then below is a detailed explanation of what this means. If you answered false to most questions, then read the description for what a low response means. An average score considers both low and high traits, so therefore you should read that description.

HIGH (mostly false)	If you answered mostly false then you are prone to hostile behaviour. You become resentful, agitated and somewhat aggressive in a situation. You tend to get angry when something doesn't go your way of feel as though you have been cheated out of something. Having a high hostile level means that you are incapable of handling your emotions. You act before you think and show little remorse during or after the event. Whilst having some levels of hostility shows passion and ambition, it also shows bluntness, bitterness and belligerence. You need to be able to handle your emotions and express them only when necessary. Employers will not stand for hostile behaviour in a work environment and it is important for everyone to feel comfortable and at ease, without having to deal with aggressive behaviour.
AVERAGE	An average score for hostility means that you show different traits from both the high and low scoring system. Overall, your personality comes across as quite capable and willing to get on with the tasks that you are set. You show little apprehension, resentment or attitude if you are given a task that you don't particularly want; you simply get on with what needs to be done. However, sometimes you have the tendency to act before you think. Sometimes this might come across as slightly rude or hostile, even though it may just be your way of conveying your enthusiasm and passion in regards to your work. Employers like to be able to see employees who are capable of getting along with people in the workforce without causing heated arguments and confrontations. On the other hand, employers don't like to see someone who is completely robust and silent. They like to see employees are capable of expressing their passion and interest on a particular matter and who are able to view their feelings and concerns when necessary.

LOW (mostly true)	If you answered mostly true to these questions, it means that you have a low hostility. You don't become agitated or angry and often keep your emotions and thoughts to yourself. You tend to get on with set tasks with little complaint and show a calm and composed state of mind. You are capable of getting on with things with no drama, no tension and no resentment. It shows you have a willingness to get on with tasks without causing a scene or getting overly worked up. Whilst having a low hostility level is mostly seen as a good thing, a very low score could suggest that you lack interest or passion. You need to be able to show your interest in something without the need to become agitated or hostile.

DEPRESSION

Depression is a state of mind that a lot of people have to deal with. It is a feeling of aversion and discontent that affects day-to-day activities and lifestyles. It often affects a person's work ethic, emotions, behaviour and their overall sense of well-being.

People that score low on depression tend to feel fine within themselves. They tend to be free from these depressive feelings such as sadness and are able to keep themselves motivated and content within the work environment. People who score high on depression are people that often lack energy, have difficulty initiating activity, and often feel down, discouraged and dejected.

A workplace likes employees to be able to handle their emotions. Employers like to be assured of the fact that they have employees that are able to get on with their jobs without emotional integrity getting in the way. They like people who tend to keep their private lives separate from their work lives to ensure maximum work ethic in the work environment.

These 30 questions will measure your level of depression and help to gain an overview of your level of neuroticism. The questions are simple; circle your answer to the statements provided.

**Note: Reversed means that answering 'true' to the question will result in a low score of that trait.**

1. I often idealise others.

True	False

2. Sometimes, I feel like I have no reason to get out of bed in the morning.

True	False

3. I always keep my feelings to myself. (Reversed)

True	False

4. I nearly always feel "empty".

True	False

5. I get very paranoid when I am on my own.

True	False

6. Sometimes I feel really disconnected with the rest of the world.

| True | False |

7. I often feel a sudden change in my mood.

| True | False |

8. I am afraid that others will leave me on my own.

| True | False |

9. I have thought about self-harm.

| True | False |

10. I find it difficult to sleep at night.

| True | False |

11. I lack motivation.

| True | False |

12. I keep my private life separate from my work life. (Reversed)

| True | False |

13. I often feel irritable or upset.

| True | False |

14. I find it hard to concentrate.

| True | False |

15. I feel restless most of the time and cannot relax.

| True | False |

16. I find it difficult to switch my mind off at night.

| True | False |

17. I feel like a failure.

| True | False |

18. I get on with the tasks I am set without complaint. (Reversed)

| True | False |

19. I feel down even when something good happens to me.

True	False

20. I feel confined and imprisoned.

True	False

21. I feel as though I am free to do what I want. (Reversed)

True	False

22. I am satisfied with who I am. (Reversed)

True	False

23. I feel jealous of the people around me.

True	False

24. I feel like I am being judged all of the time.

True	False

25. Sometimes, I feel like I am pressured to change who I am.

True	False

26. I find it difficult to interact with the others around me.

True	False

27. I find myself thinking about what my life could have been like if things were different.

True	False

28. I feel my friends and family are always here for me. (Reversed)

True	False

29. I doubt myself a lot.

True	False

30. I feel like if I was someone different, my life would be better.

True	False

Scoring System:

Circle the letter that represents your chosen answer:

Note: make sure you circle the opposite answer from your above answer for the Reversed answers

1. T / F	**2.** T / F	**3.** T / F (R)	**4.** T / F	**5.** T / F
6. T / F	**7.** T / F	**8.** T / F	**9.** T / F	**10.** T / F
11. T / F	**12.** T / F (R)	**13.** T / F	**14.** T / F	**15.** T / F
16. T / F	**17.** T / F	**18.** T / F (R)	**19.** T / F	**20.** T / F
21. T / F (R)	**22.** T / F (R)	**23.** T / F	**24.** T / F	**25.** T / F
26. T / F	**27.** T / F	**28.** T / F (R)	**29.** T / F	**30.** T / F

SCORE TOTAL:	True = ...	HIGH
SCORE TOTAL:	False = ...	LOW

Understanding Your Scores:

Your results on the Depression test will help determine your overall outcome for the trait of Neuroticism. Once you've added up how many questions you answered true to, and how many questions you answered false, it will be a clear way of distinguishing if your score was high, average or low.

If you answered true to most of the questions, then below is a detailed explanation of what this means. If you answered false to most questions, then read the description for what a low response means. An average score considers both low and high traits, so therefore you should read that description.

HIGH (mostly true)	If you answered true to most of the questions, it means you are bordering a high score for Depression. Your results demonstrate a lack of self-esteem, ambition, dejection and sadness. Whether you have experienced something saddening and influential in the past, or whether it is a phase of emotional turmoil, you are showing high levels of dissatisfaction and discouragement with the person you are. Think about talking to someone. Putting your emotions across to someone often helps people in stressful situations and offers a way of support and comfort. It also offers the first step to dealing with your issues and resolving them. Having a high level of depression often affects a person's work ethic. Therefore, it is wise to deal with your issues before they become worse. Employers want to see employees with a great work ethic, who are focused and overall, happy within the work environment, and although employers are understanding that this is an illness and not something you choose, they can help. Seek out advice or talk to someone to resolve your issues.
AVERAGE	If you answered a near equal score for high and low, it shows you have an average level for the feeling of depression. Whilst the majority of the time you appear to be content and free from depressive feelings, some of the questions you answered suggests that you possibly carry a few traits in regards to showing signs of depression. Maybe you experience negative feelings, or often feel in emotional turmoil. These factors might indicate that you are dissatisfied and find it difficult to keep focused. While employers are often sympathetic to a person's personal circumstances, you do not want to be in a position where you find yourself showing great levels of depression. Therefore, you need to focus on dealing with any personal issues before they become a wider problem in the workforce.

LOW (mostly false)	If you answered false for most of the questions, it demonstrates that you have a low depression score. This means that you are satisfied and content with the person you are and the way your life is panning out. Although you may deal with distressing and upsetting situations, you keep your feelings bottled up and get on with your work. You are seldom confronted with these depressive feelings. Having a low score for depression allows employers to be assured of happy employees who are less likely to feel discouraged. Although you may be free from depressive feelings, take into consideration other people. Other people, especially in your workplace may be going through something that you are unaware of. Try to lend a helping hand to people less fortunate than you and offer help to people who suffer from depression. They will be grateful to know a strong-minded person is there to help. Consider other people's feelings as well as looking after your own, to ensure an efficient and well-rounded workplace.

SELF-CONSCIOUSNESS

Self-consciousness is another trait that forms part of our neurotic behaviour. Self-consciousness is an acute sense of self-awareness and insecurities. Individuals who are self-conscious are often sensitive and shy in social situations. It is often linked to anxiety issues. People who are anxious about something tend to be self-conscious; they often worry about what people may think of them.

Self-conscious people are afraid of the possible thought of rejection or ridicule. They feel uncomfortable and reluctant around others. They fear that others will criticise, laugh or joke about them which constitutes the feelings of awkwardness and apprehension.

People who score highly on the self-consciousness test are the people who feel all of the above. They worry about what people may think, they are anxious about what people might say, they feel awkward in social situations. Generally, they display high levels of anxiety and are prone to traits such as vulnerability, low self-esteem and lack of confidence.

In contrast, people who score low do not suffer from these traits. They tend to be people who are laid back, confident and content with who they are. They do not suffer from nerves in social situations, they do not mistake the impression that people are watching and judging them. They feel comfortable and at ease with the people around them.

These 30 questions will measure your level of self-consciousness and help to gain an overview of your level of neuroticism. The questions are simple; circle your answer to the statements provided.

__Note: Reversed means that answering 'true' to the question will result in a low score of that trait.__

1. I am generally attentive to my inner feelings.

True	False

2. I never scrutinise myself. (Reversed)

True	False

3. Generally, I'm not very aware of myself.

True	False

4. I am self-conscious about the way I look.

True	False

5. I am concerned with what other people think of me.

True	False

6. I look after the way I look, so people won't judge me.

True	False

7. I worry about making a good impression.

True	False

8. I spend a lot of time in the morning deciding what to wear.

True	False

9. Sometimes, I feel ugly.

True	False

10. I look at others and wished I looked like that.

True	False

11. I become nervous when someone is looking at me.

True	False

12. I am the leader of my group. (Reversed)

True	False

13. I tend to withdraw from large crowds.

True	False

14. I get embarrassed easily.

True	False

15. Sometimes I feel like I don't belong.

True	False

16. I am usually thinking of others. (Reversed)

True	False

17. I sometimes step back in order to look at myself from a distance.

True	False

18. I think about myself a lot.

| True | False |

19. I care a lot about how I present myself to others around me.

| True | False |

20. It takes me a while to interact with my peers.

| True | False |

21. I find it easy to talk to strangers. (Reversed)

| True | False |

22. I get nervous when I speak in public.

| True | False |

23. I take pride in my appearance.

| True | False |

24. I generally feel unhappy with myself.

| True | False |

25. I often try to imagine myself differently.

| True | False |

26. I envy my friends and family.

| True | False |

27. I always scrutinise myself.

| True | False |

28. What others think of me is no concern of mine. (Reversed)

| True | False |

29. I throw any clothes on in the morning; I don't care what I look like. (Reversed)

| True | False |

30. Generally, I feel anxious, awkward and shy.

| True | False |

Scoring System:

Circle the letter that represents your chosen answer:

Note: make sure you circle the opposite answer from your above answer for the Reversed answers

1.	T / F	2. (R)	T / F	3.	T / F	4.	T / F	5.	T / F
6.	T / F	7.	T / F	8.	T / F	9.	T / F	10.	T / F
11.	T / F	12. (R)	T / F	13.	T / F	14.	T / F	15.	T / F
16. (R)	T / F	17.	T / F	18.	T / F	19.	T / F	20.	T / F
21. (R)	T / F	22.	T / F	23.	T / F	24.	T / F	25.	T / F
26.	T / F	27.	T / F	28. (R)	T / F	29. (R)	T / F	30.	T / F

SCORE TOTAL:	True =	....	HIGH
SCORE TOTAL:	False =	....	LOW

Understanding Your Scores:

Your results on the Self-Consciousness test will help determine your overall outcome for the trait of Neuroticism. Once you've added up how many questions you answered true to, and how many questions you answered false, it will be a clear way of distinguishing if your score was high, average or low.

If you answered true to most of the questions, then below is a detailed explanation of what this means. If you answered false to most questions, then read the description for what a low response means. An average score considers both low and high traits, so therefore you should read that description.

HIGH (mostly true)	Scoring a high mark on the Self-Consciousness test suggests that you are quite self-conscious with who you are. You tend to withdraw from large crowds and find it difficult to interact in social situations. You often feel as though you are being judged or ridiculed and therefore this makes you feel shy, awkward and reserved. People who experience high levels of self-consciousness often experience high levels of anxiety issues. You are afraid to be yourself; you get the impression that people are watching your every move. Employers prefer people with an average score regarding self-consciousness. They like people who are not afraid to be themselves. They like people who can interact and get along with others without feeling inferior to them. Try and work on your self-esteem by engaging with your issues, rather than avoiding them. For example, if you are self-conscious about the way you look, try looking at yourself from another perspective. Or simply talk to someone, more likely than not someone else is experiencing the same thing you are.
AVERAGE	An average score for self-consciousness means that you are borderline both the high and low boundaries. Overall, you are quite content with who you are. You're not overly confident but you don't suffer major self-belief issues. You may get nervous at times, but you don't let this become an issue or stop you from doing something you want to do. You show both levels of self-awareness and self-consciousness. You are aware of the type of person you want to be and are not afraid to be yourself, but you sometimes withdraw from awkward social situations.

	Employers take pride in employing people who are not afraid to be themselves. They like people who show confidence and integrity as well as nerves and apprehension. It makes them believe that you are human. Everybody gets nervous and feels self-conscious, but it is how you present yourself to them that makes them believe in your abilities and skills. Don't be afraid to show a little self-consciousness but also a little self-assurance.
LOW (mostly false)	If you scored a low mark it means that you do not suffer from self-conscious issues. You're the type of person who feels comfortable with who they are. You do not get nervous interacting with large groups of people and you don't carry the fears of being judged or ridiculed. You simply get on with what needs to be done and do not worry about how you are perceived. Generally, you are more self-aware than self-conscious. Although you might take pride in your appearance, and like to impress others around you, you do not threat about it. You do not become succumbed into the impression that you are being watched. However, although having a lower score is more beneficial, you do not want to come across as arrogant or self-centred. You want to maintain a level of composure and confidence, whilst not showing superiority or a huge ego. Getting a balanced score for self-consciousness is most constructive. It demonstrates that you're not scared to be yourself, but you do show some concern of how you interact and come across to other people.

IMPULSIVENESS

An impulse is a construction that allows a person to act on a whim and generally, not think about what they are about to say or do. Impulsiveness has the tendency to illustrate characteristics of a person that shows little consideration or no forethought about the consequences of their actions. Impulse actions are often poorly judged. They are premature thoughts that often result in somewhat undesirable consequences. Impulsive people usually have the traits of quickness, courageousness, boldness and spontaneity.

People with high impulse levels act quickly in response. They show little knowledge or understanding of deliberation. It demonstrates to employers a person's ability to act in a quick manner and use their initiative and independence; something employers admire in their workforce. However, employers may have to deal with impulsive people and encounter the consequences from that person's actions. A person who scores a low mark on the impulsiveness tests demonstrates a carefully considered thought process and delays gratification.

You want to be able to maintain a level of impulsiveness for quick responses, a quick work ethic and independent thinking as well as understanding that your actions have consequences.

These 30 questions will measure your level of impulsiveness and help gain an overview of your level of neuroticism. The questions are simple; circle your answer to the statements provided.

Note: Reversed means that answering 'true' to the question will result in a high score of that trait.

1. I usually think before I speak.

True	False

2. I am a cautious person.

True	False

3. I over analyse most things.

True	False

4. I take into consideration other people's feelings.

True	False

5. I look at something from all angles.

| True | False |

6. I like to stop and think before I do something.

| True | False |

7. I worry about the outcome.

| True | False |

8. I have trouble controlling my impulses. (Reversed)

| True | False |

9. I follow a sensible approach.

| True | False |

10. I like to plan ahead.

| True | False |

11. I get on with things quickly so I know that they are done. (Reversed)

| True | False |

12. I have a reserved attitude towards everything I do.

| True | False |

13. I consider all the possibilities.

| True | False |

14. I act upon my feelings. (Reversed)

| True | False |

15. I always look at the consequences of my actions.

| True | False |

16. I have a careful approach for everything I do.

| True | False |

17. Sometimes I do something without knowing what I am doing. (Reversed)

| True | False |

18. I like to use my time as efficiently as I can.

| True | False |

19. I like to know what I am doing before I start something.

| True | False |

20. I am a reserved person.

| True | False |

21. People who act out on a whim annoy me.

| True | False |

22. I think people who act quickly are unprepared.

| True | False |

23. I consider myself an organised person.

| True | False |

24. I generally don't like taking blame for something that's gone wrong.

| True | False |

25. I try to avoid making mistakes by planning ahead.

| True | False |

26. Sometimes, I want to 'do' it instead of 'think' about it. (Reversed)

| True | False |

27. Always be prepared.

| True | False |

28. There is no such thing as over preparation.

| True | False |

29. I value a rational approach.

| True | False |

30. I don't usually blurt things out unless I've considered them carefully.

| True | False |

Scoring System:

Circle the letter that represents your chosen answer:

Note: make sure you circle the opposite answer from your above answer for the Reversed answers

1.	T / F	**2.**	T / F	**3.**	T / F	**4.**	T / F	**5.**	T / F
6.	T / F	**7.**	T / F	**8.** (R)	T / F	**9.**	T / F	**10.**	T / F
11. (R)	T / F	**12.**	T / F	**13.**	T / F	**14.** (R)	T / F	**15.**	T / F
16.	T / F	**17.** (R)	T / F	**18.**	T / F	**19.**	T / F	**20.**	T / F
21.	T / F	**22.**	T / F	**23.**	T / F	**24.**	T / F	**25.**	T / F
26. (R)	T / F	**27.**	T / F	**28.**	T / F	**29.**	T / F	**30.**	T / F

SCORE TOTAL:	True =	....	LOW
SCORE TOTAL:	False =	....	HIGH

Understanding Your Scores:

Your results on the Impulsiveness test will help determine your overall outcome for the trait of Neuroticism. Once you've added up how many questions you answered true to, and how many questions you answered false, it will be a clear way of distinguishing if your score was high, average or low.

If you answered true to most of the questions, then below is a detailed explanation of what this means. If you answered false to most questions, then read the description for what a low response means. An average score considers both low and high traits, so therefore you should read that description.

HIGH (mostly false)	If you answered false to most of the questions, it suggests that you are more likely to act on impulse and therefore have a high impulsiveness level. You rarely stop to think about your actions. You just do it! You feel strong urges to demonstrate your ability to be able to act in a time efficient manner. People with high impulsiveness tend to be guided by the thoughts of short term rewards, rather than long-term effects. This can be costly for any type of business. If a person has an extreme impulse score, it might suggest that they are less likely to stop and take into consideration the possible effects and consequences of their actions. A person with an extreme high score might want to consider alternative approaches. Try and take into consideration several possibilities and don't just dive into action. Stop and think about what your choices mean for any business and how this might help or jeopardise a particular situation.
AVERAGE	If you answered a more average score between both the high and low boundaries, it means you showed high and low characteristics of impulsiveness. You are quite a rational and sensible person who shows careful considerations in regards to making decisions or coming up with solutions. You like to test your knowledge and use that as your basis for your reasoning and logic. However, sometimes you may dive into a situation if the situation requires you to do so, therefore displaying your versatility. This is something every employer likes to see in their workforce. They like to maintain a workforce who are not only able to think on their feet, but are cautious and considerate about the possible consequences that may lie ahead.

LOW (mostly true)	If you answered true to most of the questions, it means you have a low impulsiveness level. You demonstrate a rational and sensible approach for most things and are cautious of the outcome. You don't tend to act on impulse or urge, you take your time to carefully consider the possibilities and understand what it means for you and the consequences it could lead to. You tend not to overindulge and are therefore less likely to act on a whim, these are the types of people employers often like to see. They like to see a level of maturity and knowledge of knowing when to act and when to hold back. Although, having an extreme low score suggests that you are unable to think by yourself. That you are unable to act on something without guidance and can therefore be a problem. You want to maintain an average level of impulse and to know when to act quickly if a situation requires.

How Neurotic Are You?

So, you've finished answering all the questions on Neuroticism. We have provided the table below to generate a general understanding of your level of neuroticism.

Now go back through the six sub-traits for Neuroticism and use your high, average and low scores to fill in the table below.

TRAIT	Anxiety	Vulnera-bility	Hostility	Depres-sion	Self-Con-sciousness	Impulsive-ness
HIGH, AVERAGE OR LOW?						

What does this mean overall?

HIGH	If you scored mostly high for each sub-section, it means you are bordering high levels of Neuroticism. A high level of Neuroticism means that you experience more than one of the attributes explored throughout the chapter (i.e. anxiety, hostility depression etc).
	People who score highly are often emotionally reactive. This means that you are extremely sensitive and volatile, demonstrating emotional instability.
	You tend to feel inferior to others; you often feel awkward, shy, nervous and vulnerable in social situations and find it difficult to be yourself.
	A high level of Neuroticism can often affect a person's way of thinking, their behaviour and their feelings. Quite often, a person with high levels of neuroticism feels hopeless and frustrated with themselves, and often takes it out on others.
	TRAITS = anxious, moody, irritable, hostile, vulnerable, jittery, bitterness, discouraged

AVERAGE	If you scored an average score overall in the Neurotic test, it means that you show both traits for high neurotic and low neuroticism. You often appear in control of your emotions. You tend to keep your feelings bottled up the best you can and try not to let personal problems get in the way of your work. However, most people are prone to the occasionally step back or upset. You may experience sadness and emotional turmoil occasionally, but you try to limit how much of it you show at your work. Whilst you may show some levels of vulnerability, you come across as a strong, independent and capable person who tends to not let their feelings interfere with their work. **TRAITS = vulnerability but strong, discouraged but hopeful, doubtful but optimistic**
LOW	If you scored mostly low for each sub-section, it means you are bordering a low level of Neuroticism. This means that you are less likely to feel upset or anxious and less emotionally reactive. In other words, you are more emotionally stable and demonstrate a high level of calmness, rational and capability at dealing with your emotions. Whilst being emotionally stable is more of an advantage, you do not want to come across as a person who doesn't take their work seriously or not interested in their work. You want to be able to show some level of empathy and charisma to reinforce your passion and enthusiasm regarding your work. A low score suggests a person to be freer of negative feelings, if not free they are able to keep their feelings under control and not let their personal life interfere with their work life. **TRAITS = confident, optimistic, emotionally stable, calm, relaxed, even tempered**

What does this say to employers about your personality?

A person who can control their feelings and emotions is a person that employers prefer. Employers seek to find employees who have a great work ethic, despite any personal problems. Of course, employers are sympathetic to such feelings, we are all human, but it is how you deal with the situation and how you handle yourself in difficult times that employers want to see.

Thus, for this test, you don't want your score to be extremely high or extremely low, but somewhere in between, ideally more closely to the lower bracket. This will reinforce your emotional stability and tell employers that you are a strong, poised, reliable person for the job.

CHAPTER 2 - The Big 5:

Agreeableness

CHAPTER 2 - THE BIG 5: AGREEABLENESS

Another aspect of The Big 5 model of personality is agreeableness. Agreeableness is a personality trait that reflects a person's individual behaviour in regards to empathy, cooperation and consideration. It reflects an individual's attempt to engage in social harmony and how they interact with the others around them.

A person who is high in agreeableness is empathetic, generous, helpful and willing to compromise their interests for others. They tend to have an optimistic view of human nature and are able to believe that people can be honest, trustworthy and sincere.

People that score a low mark on agreeableness tends to struggle with letting people in and trusting them. They are people who are characterised by scepticism. In other words, they are wary about other people around them. These people have the tendency to be manipulative in social engagements and are not afraid to engage in confrontation.

Agreeableness is obviously an advantageous attribute to have within the workplace. Agreeable people are less likely to cause conflict and more likely to get on with the people around them and therefore able to create a calm and comfortable atmosphere. However, some level of disagreeableness can be considered as beneficial. Some tasks require you to think on your feet and make absolute and tough decisions. It is important that you are able to show both levels of agreeableness in order to maintain an active and sufficient workplace.

Several sub-traits can be assessed in personality tests to measure agreeableness. These indicate how agreeable you are which can be analysed in terms of **trust, straightforwardness, modesty, compliance, altruism and tender-mindedness.**

In this chapter, it will focus on each one of these terms and assess your personality to examine the extent to which you show levels of agreeableness.

TRUST

One of the traits of assessing a person's agreeableness is trust. Trust is the ability to hold firm reliance on faith, honesty and trustworthiness. To be trusting in someone or something, a person has to believe in that someone or something. Some people find it difficult to trust others, whilst others trust too easily.

A person who scores highly on the trust test is considered somewhat naïve. You do not want to give the impression that you trust everything you hear or see as stone hard fact. A person with a high score in trust assumes most people to be honest and have good intentions.

Someone who scores a low mark on the trust test finds it difficult to trust others. They may see others as threatening, devious and selfish. People who lack trust and have trouble showing faith in someone or something are sometimes said to show levels of paranoia.

You want to aim for an average score. For management and business-orientated positions, having complete trust in something or someone can be seen as naïve and irresponsible. Thus, you want to show experience and maturity. However, positions in service-orientated roles, you want to show high levels of trust in order to maintain a healthy and comfortable work environment with others around you.

These 30 questions will measure your level of trust and help to determine your level of agreeableness. The questions are simple; use the table below to answer the following questions. Circle the number that represents your answer and then use your answers to check your score.

__Note: Reversed means that answering 'agree' or 'strongly agree' to the question will result in a low score of that trait.__

1	2	3	4	5
Strongly Disagree	Disagree	Neutral	Agree	Strongly Agree

1.   I usually believe what people tell me.

1	2	3	4	5

2.   I am always honest.

1	2	3	4	5

3.   I sometimes lie to get what I want. (Reversed)

1	2	3	4	5

4.   I consider myself a reliable and trustworthy person.

1	2	3	4	5

5. I tend to find fault in others. (Reversed)

1	2	3	4	5

6. I am helpful and unselfish working with others.

1	2	3	4	5

7. I think of others before myself.

1	2	3	4	5

8. I never start confrontations.

1	2	3	4	5

9. I get on with the work I am asked and do not question it.

1	2	3	4	5

10. I tend to be the friendly one.

1	2	3	4	5

11. I am considerate and kind to everyone.

1	2	3	4	5

12. I have trust issues. (Reversed)

1	2	3	4	5

13. I think of myself before others. (Reversed)

1	2	3	4	5

14. I like to cooperate with others.

1	2	3	4	5

15. I work best in a team.

1	2	3	4	5

16. I avoid getting in disputes at work.

1	2	3	4	5

17. People often take advantage of those who are friendly and honest. (Reversed)

1	2	3	4	5

18. I don't often trust others. (Reversed)

1	2	3	4	5

19. I don't believe that people would talk behind my back.

1	2	3	4	5

20. I dislike heated arguments.

1	2	3	4	5

21. I work best with people I can trust.

1	2	3	4	5

22. Trusting someone comes easily to me.

1	2	3	4	5

23. Don't judge a book by its cover; they might surprise you.

1	2	3	4	5

24. I have no reason to doubt people who tell me something.

1	2	3	4	5

25. Every other person I meet cannot be trusted. (Reversed)

1	2	3	4	5

26. I hardly ever feel uncertain or doubtful about things.

1	2	3	4	5

27. I never feel betrayed.

1	2	3	4	5

28. I would rather agree than argue.

1	2	3	4	5

29. I don't like to disagree with what others have to say.

1	2	3	4	5

30. People who are extremely friendly, raise my suspicions. (Reversed)

1	2	3	4	5

Scoring System:

Circle the number that represents your chosen answer:

Note: make sure you circle the opposite answer from your above answer for the Reversed answers

1.	2.	3.	4.	5.
1 2 3 4 5	1 2 3 4 5	(R) 1 2 3 4 5	1 2 3 4 5	(R) 1 2 3 4 5
6.	**7.**	**8.**	**9.**	**10.**
1 2 3 4 5	1 2 3 4 5	1 2 3 4 5	1 2 3 4 5	1 2 3 4 5
11.	**12.**	**13.**	**14.**	**15.**
1 2 3 4 5	(R) 1 2 3 4 5	(R) 1 2 3 4 5	1 2 3 4 5	1 2 3 4 5
16.	**17.**	**18.**	**19.**	**20.**
1 2 3 4 5	(R) 1 2 3 4 5	(R) 1 2 3 4 5	1 2 3 4 5	1 2 3 4 5
21.	**22.**	**23.**	**24.**	**25.**
1 2 3 4 5	1 2 3 4 5	1 2 3 4 5	1 2 3 4 5	(R) 1 2 3 4 5
26.	**27.**	**28.**	**29.**	**30.**
1 2 3 4 5	1 2 3 4 5	1 2 3 4 5	1 2 3 4 5	(R) 1 2 3 4 5

SCORE TOTAL:	1's =	....	LOW
SCORE TOTAL:	2's =	....	
SCORE TOTAL:	3's =	....	AVERAGE
SCORE TOTAL:	4's =	....	
SCORE TOTAL:	5's =	....	HIGH

Circle your highest score.

Understanding Your Scores:

Your results on the Trust test will help determine your overall outcome for the trait of Agreeableness. Once you've added up how many questions you answered strongly disagree, disagree, neutral, agree and strongly agree; it will be a clear way of distinguishing if your score was high, average or low.

If you answered mostly 5's or 4's, your score is going to demonstrate an extremely high level of trust. If you answered mostly 1's or 2's, your score is going to be extremely low. If you scored mostly 3's, you should read the average column.

HIGH (mostly 5's or 4's)	If you scored mostly 5's on your trust test, it demonstrates an extremely high level of trust. You are the type of person who is able to put your trust in someone or something very easily and not question the motives behind it. Although being trusting is an admirable quality is can be undesirable. Being trusting allows you to provide a comfortable and calm workplace without little arguments or dispute. You are able to get along with people easily. You accept everything as truth that has good intentions and little room for disagreement. Being too trusting can come across as quite naïve and inexperienced. You cannot accept everything as hard core fact. You need to take into consideration the possibilities of other decisions or possible thesis. You want to aim your score so that you show some level of trust, but some level of the ability to question something that might not necessarily be correct.
AVERAGE (mostly 3's)	Scoring an average score on the trust test suggests that although you are often trusting, you sometimes have your doubts. You are able to trust people to some extent; mostly these people you trust, you have known for a while. You may struggle to trust people at the beginning, but once you get to know them, you are able to feel comfortable and trusting in their company. However, you are the type of person that cannot trust everyone. You sometimes have your reservations about people. You may not know why or it may be because you don't really know them; but you tend to withdraw slightly from these people until you get to know them better. Employers like to see their workforce are able to trust one another in order to provide a healthy and stable working environment. However, employers also like to see employees who are capable of judging characters, particularly if they are doing something wrong or something they are not meant to be doing. Employers like to see employees have the capability and integrity to come forward in moments like this and express their concerns.

LOW (mostly 1's or 2's)	If you scored mostly 1's on your trust test, it suggests an extremely low level of trust. You find it difficult to accept something as the truth and struggle to receive information as accurate. You are the type of person who is cautious and very sceptical about other people's motives or intentions and therefore find it difficult to maintain healthy social relationships. Having an extreme low score of trust suggests a person to be paranoid. It makes it hard to create a comfortable work environment with untrusting people, due to lack of motivation and awkwardness. You want to assure that your persona comes across as somewhat trusting but somewhat cautious. You want to be able to show employers that you can think on your feet and put across other possible ideas, but also to show a certain level of respect to trust what someone has said or done in order to provide maximum business potential and a healthy work environment.

STRAIGHTFORWARDNESS

Another way of assessing a person's agreeableness is to determine how straightforward a person is. The term straightforwardness can be used to describe someone who often displays frankness in their expressions. They are straight to the point; they are the people who often have something to say. They are people who are honest and open about their emotions and are often quite direct and undeviating.

People who score a low mark on the straightforwardness test are usually people who are often guarded in terms of their feelings and emotions. They believe that a certain level of deception in social relationships is sometimes necessary and therefore do not provide an account of the whole truth.

Scoring a high mark on the straightforwardness test suggests a person to be widely open about their emotions and are not afraid to share what they are feeling.

To employers, straightforwardness is not all that straightforward. It is difficult to find the right balance of how straightforward a person should be. You do not want to come across as stubborn or inflexible, but are able to speak their mind and express their views.

These 30 questions will measure your level of straightforwardness and help to determine your level of agreeableness. The questions are simple; use the table below to answer the following questions. Circle the number that represents your answer and then use your answers to check your score.

Note: Reversed means that answering 'agree' or 'strongly agree' to the question will result in a low score of that trait.

1	2	3	4	5
Strongly Disagree	Disagree	Neutral	Agree	Strongly Agree

1. I have no problem correcting people if they are mistaken.

1	2	3	4	5

2. If other people disagree, I rarely change my mind to satisfy them.

1	2	3	4	5

3. I don't wander away from my beliefs, despite other people disagreeing.

1	2	3	4	5

4. I am cautious to express my concerns. (Reversed)

1	2	3	4	5

5. I speak my mind all the time.

1	2	3	4	5

6. I am often direct with the people around me.

1	2	3	4	5

7. I stand firm with my opinions and beliefs.

1	2	3	4	5

8. 'My way or the highway'.

1	2	3	4	5

9. I will not change my mind about important things even if others tell me otherwise.

1	2	3	4	5

10. If someone disagrees with me, I look at it from their point of view. (Reversed)

1	2	3	4	5

11. The freedom to say and do what I want is very important to me.

1	2	3	4	5

12. I can't imagine a situation where I would go against what I believe.

1	2	3	4	5

13. I refuse to do things that I do not agree with.

1	2	3	4	5

14. I say exactly what I think.

1	2	3	4	5

15. Seldom, I will have a dispute with someone over different beliefs to mine. (Reversed)

1	2	3	4	5

16. I respect the right to speak my mind in every situation.

1	2	3	4	5

17. I hardly ever voice my opinion in case it is wrong. (Reversed)

1	2	3	4	5

18. I have no problem telling people an alternative option.

1	2	3	4	5

19. I prefer being direct.

1	2	3	4	5

20. I don't like it when people constantly change their mind to satisfy others.

1	2	3	4	5

21. I avoid telling the truth so it doesn't hurt other people's feelings. (Reversed)

1	2	3	4	5

22. I tend to think things through before saying something. (Reversed)

1	2	3	4	5

23. It is important for me to speak my mind.

1	2	3	4	5

24. I would never stray away from my values.

1	2	3	4	5

25. I often come across as stubborn.

1	2	3	4	5

26. I see no reason to beat around the bush; directness is best.

1	2	3	4	5

27. I often speak before I think.

1	2	3	4	5

28. Being direct comes across as arrogant and rude. (Reversed)

1	2	3	4	5

29. I change my view according to who I am with. (Reversed)

1	2	3	4	5

30. I consider myself an honest person who likes to speak their mind.

1	2	3	4	5

Scoring System:

Circle the number that represents your chosen answer:

Note: make sure you circle the opposite answer from your above answer for the Reversed answers

1.	2.	3.	4.	5.
1 2 3 4 5	1 2 3 4 5	1 2 3 4 5	*(R)* 1 2 3 4 5	1 2 3 4 5
6.	7.	8.	9.	10.
1 2 3 4 5	1 2 3 4 5	1 2 3 4 5	1 2 3 4 5	*(R)* 1 2 3 4 5
11.	12.	13.	14.	15.
1 2 3 4 5	1 2 3 4 5	1 2 3 4 5	1 2 3 4 5	*(R)* 1 2 3 4 5
16.	17.	18.	19.	20.
1 2 3 4 5	*(R)* 1 2 3 4 5	1 2 3 4 5	1 2 3 4 5	1 2 3 4 5
21.	22.	23.	24.	25.
(R) 1 2 3 4 5	*(R)* 1 2 3 4 5	1 2 3 4 5	1 2 3 4 5	1 2 3 4 5
26.	27.	28.	29.	30.
1 2 3 4 5	1 2 3 4 5	*(R)* 1 2 3 4 5	*(R)* 1 2 3 4 5	1 2 3 4 5

SCORE TOTAL:	1's =	....	LOW
SCORE TOTAL:	2's =	....	
SCORE TOTAL:	3's =	....	AVERAGE
SCORE TOTAL:	4's =	....	
SCORE TOTAL:	5's =	....	HIGH

Circle your highest score.

Understanding Your Scores:

Your results on the Straightforwardness test will help determine your overall outcome for the trait of Agreeableness. Once you've added up how many questions you answered strongly disagree, disagree, neutral, agree and strongly agree; it will be a clear way of distinguishing if your score was high, average or low.

If you answered mostly 5's or 4's, your score is going to demonstrate an extremely high level of trust. If you answered mostly 1's or 2's, your score is going to be extremely low. If you scored mostly 3's, you should read the average column.

HIGH (mostly 5's or 4's)	If you scored mostly 5's in the straightforwardness test, it means that you have an extremely high straightforward approach.

You tend not to hold back your opinions or feelings and like to put your views across.

You proceed in straight manner, you are direct, firm and undeviating. You like to be able to say what you think in a clear and concise manner.

Being straightforward can be an advantage. It allows for quick responses and independent thinking to be established, which can be beneficial for businesses. Employers like to know that they have employees who can think on their feet and put across their views and ideas. Not only does it make that person look experienced and know what they're talking about, but demonstrates a high level of independence.

However, being extremely straightforward can come across as rude, arrogant and stubborn. So, you want to make sure that you show levels of straightforwardness but not over exaggerate or indulge in undesirable traits such as stubbornness. |
| **AVERAGE (mostly 3's)** | An average score for straightforwardness means that you borderline both the high and low scoring boundaries.

You come across as direct and straightforward. You are not afraid to express what you think, and you like your voice to be heard.

Sometimes, you have the tendency to struggle putting your views across in certain situations. Maybe because you have nothing to say or maybe you feel slightly inferior to those around you.

Although you are direct and affirmative, you also place caution when necessary. You cannot jump into every situation in the same way; therefore your approach needs to be adapted accordingly. |

LOW (mostly 1's or 2's)	If you scored mostly 1's in the straightforwardness test, it means that you have an extremely low approach in regards to forth thinking and directness.

You struggle to put your views across in social situations and often think about your actions before you do something.

You do not act on impulse. You're a cautious person who carefully considers lots of possibilities.

Scoring an extremely low mark in regards to directness and straightforwardness; suggests you are guarded. You guard your emotions and ideas and keep them bottled up.

Employers like to see a person who can act on instinct, be able to share ideas and put across their views. Not being able to express their ideas and opinions, not only shows lack of independent thinking, but also suggests you take little interest in the matter.

You should aim to be able to show a straightforward approach in order to create a highly sufficient work ethic. Most businesses look for candidates who are able to think for themselves as well as with a team. Gain confidence with your ideas and express yourself in social situations – you never know, you might come up with an idea that is followed through and put into action! |

MODESTY

Another sub-trait that can be analysed in terms of agreeableness is Modesty. Most people on a personality test, despite the position that they are applying for try to present themselves as a modest person. However, for this test you want to be able to show a balanced level of modesty.

People who score low on modesty are those who claim that they are not better than anyone else; that they are equal. They take pride and confidence in the person they are or the abilities that they possess. They like to make people aware of their accomplishments and take the spot-light for something they have done or achieved.

High scorers are the complete opposite. They are very reserved with the person they are or what they have achieved. They do not like to boast about their accomplishments and often keep themselves to themselves.

To employers, modesty is an important trait. Depending on the position you are applying for, maintaining some level of modesty is important. For example, for sales people and managerial positions, you want to be able to convey 'self-promotion'; the job requires you to do so and so being too modest, will affect your result and suggests a lack of confidence.

You want to be able to show modesty when it is required, and 'sing your praises' when it is necessary. You don't want to over embellish in your accomplishments as this will connote arrogance and self-centredness. However, you want to be able to convey confidence and self-esteem when the situation requires you to do so.

These 30 questions will measure your level of modesty and help to determine your level of agreeableness. The questions are simple; use the table below to answer the following questions. Circle the number that represents your answer and then use your answers to check your score.

__Note: Reversed means that answering 'agree' or 'strongly agree' to the question will result in a low score of that trait.__

1	2	3	4	5
Strongly Disagree	Disagree	Neutral	Agree	Strongly Agree

1.   I consider myself a humble person.

1	2	3	4	5

2.   I don't like to boast about my accomplishments.

1	2	3	4	5

3.   Compliments embarrass me.

1	2	3	4	5

4. I like people to know what I am good at. (Reversed)

1	2	3	4	5

5. I try not to be a show off.

1	2	3	4	5

6. I know that I am good because everybody keeps telling me so. (Reversed)

1	2	3	4	5

7. Modesty doesn't become me. (Reversed)

1	2	3	4	5

8. I am essentially a modest person.

1	2	3	4	5

9. I never gloat.

1	2	3	4	5

10. I don't see the point in showing off.

1	2	3	4	5

11. Gloating gets you nowhere in life.

1	2	3	4	5

12. I don't often 'sing my own praises'.

1	2	3	4	5

13. I don't like being centre of attention.

1	2	3	4	5

14. I often talk about my accomplishments. (Reversed)

1	2	3	4	5

15. Every now and then you have to 'sing your own praises' (Reversed)

1	2	3	4	5

16. I often boast about my success. (Reversed)

1	2	3	4	5

17. If I am successful, everybody knows about it. (Reversed)

1	2	3	4	5

18. I love receiving compliments (Reversed).

1	2	3	4	5

19. Seldom, do I show off.

1	2	3	4	5

20. I consider myself self-effacing.

1	2	3	4	5

21. I don't like to stand out from the crowd.

1	2	3	4	5

22. Modesty is an admirable quality.

1	2	3	4	5

23. People who are modest are not concerned of pleasing others.

1	2	3	4	5

24. I hardly ever rejoice in my own success.

1	2	3	4	5

25. I get on with things without the need of praise.

1	2	3	4	5

26. I will show off if I get the chance. (Reversed)

1	2	3	4	5

27. I hardly ever look at myself in the mirror.

1	2	3	4	5

28. I think people who look at themselves in shop windows are vain.

1	2	3	4	5

29. I get upset when people don't notice my accomplishments. (Reversed)

1	2	3	4	5

30. Modesty comes easily to me.

1	2	3	4	5

Scoring System:

Circle the number that represents your chosen answer:

Note: make sure you circle the opposite answer from your above answer for the Reversed answers

1.	2.	3.	4.	5.
1 2 3 4 5	1 2 3 4 5	1 2 3 4 5	(R) 1 2 3 4 5	1 2 3 4 5
6. (R) 1 2 3 4 5	**7.** (R) 1 2 3 4 5	**8.** 1 2 3 4 5	**9.** 1 2 3 4 5	**10.** 1 2 3 4 5
11. 1 2 3 4 5	**12.** 1 2 3 4 5	**13.** 1 2 3 4 5	**14.** (R) 1 2 3 4 5	**15.** (R) 1 2 3 4 5
16. (R) 1 2 3 4 5	**17.** (R) 1 2 3 4 5	**18.** (R) 1 2 3 4 5	**19.** 1 2 3 4 5	**20.** 1 2 3 4 5
21. 1 2 3 4 5	**22.** 1 2 3 4 5	**23.** 1 2 3 4 5	**24.** 1 2 3 4 5	**25.** 1 2 3 4 5
26. (R) 1 2 3 4 5	**27.** 1 2 3 4 5	**28.** 1 2 3 4 5	**29.** (R) 1 2 3 4 5	**30.** 1 2 3 4 5

SCORE TOTAL:	1's =	....	LOW
SCORE TOTAL:	2's =	....	
SCORE TOTAL:	3's =	....	AVERAGE
SCORE TOTAL:	4's =	....	
SCORE TOTAL:	5's =	....	HIGH

Circle your highest score.

Understanding Your Scores:

Your results on the Modesty test will help determine your overall outcome for the trait of Agreeableness. Once you've added up how many questions you answered strongly disagree, disagree, neutral, agree and strongly agree; it will be a clear way of distinguishing if your score was high, average or low.

If you answered mostly 5's or 4's, your score is going to demonstrate an extremely high level of trust. If you answered mostly 1's or 2's, your score is going to be extremely low. If you scored mostly 3's, you should read the average column.

HIGH (mostly 5's or 4's)	If you scored mostly 5's in the modesty test, this demonstrates that you are extremely modest. An extremely modest person does not like to claim unwanted attention. You have the quality or state of mind of being unassuming to your abilities. You're the type of person who doesn't like to show off any achievements of gratification. You are free of showiness or ostentation. You are humble, reserved, and unpretentious. These personality traits are extremely valuable to employers. They like to see employees who don't seek constant needs for attention and are able to do their work to a great standard without showing off. Whilst remaining humble and modest is considered a positive, it might suggest low self-confidence or self-esteem. Thus, you want to make sure that you are able to show a good level of acknowledgement of your own work and be proud of the accomplishments you have achieved.
AVERAGE (mostly 3's)	If you scored mostly 3's in the modesty test, it shows you have an average score and show both characteristics of high and low levels of modesty. Overall, you are considered quite modest. You are humble and reserved in most things. However, you are also the type of person who likes the occasional attention about your achievements. You take pride in your accomplishments and like people to know that you are doing well. You do not however, have the need to continuously seek attention and show off. You like to feel appreciated and get rewarded for a job well done.

LOW **(mostly 1's or 2's)**	If you scored mostly 1's in the modesty test, it shows that you have extremely low levels of modesty. Low levels of modesty means that you are in no way humble or shy about making a statement of your own accomplishments and good work. You like the attention; to know that you have done well by others telling you so, you ravish the thoughts. Showing lack of modesty is something employers do not want to see. Yes they want you to feel proud of your work and yes, everyone wants to feel appreciated, but you need to understand the difference between great self-confidence and arrogance. To employers, having no modesty in your work might imply that you are somewhat arrogant and superior to others. You need to be able to show a balance of self-confidence and modest behaviour. A balance of these traits for most jobs is often desirable and therefore it is crucial you are able to demonstrate your understanding of what is required.

COMPLIANCE

Assessing a person's agreeableness, personality tests often refer to the term compliance. This facet takes into consideration a person's typical response in regards to conflict. It is a person's action or fact of obeying a wish or demand.

People who score highly on the compliance test tend to withdraw from conflict. They dislike confrontation. They obey what is asked of them. They are trusting and able to follow commands. They show cooperation in the workforce and are often willing to compromise in order to help others.

Low scorers on the compliance test are more likely to show hesitation in obeying something or someone. They are more likely to show intimidation in order to get their own way. Low scorers are more likely to show assertiveness and aggressiveness in response. They tend to be people who are suspicious and often don't like following the rules. Low scorers are often opinionated and have something to say; and instead of fulfilling and obeying something or someone, they often resist and assert their thoughts or issues on the subject matter.

Employers seek for employees who are compliant workers and trusting people. They like to be able to maintain a workforce with little disruption. Employing a person who is not compliant in the workforce makes work life difficult and uncomfortable. These people will make a scene and express their thoughts on everything and therefore show little respect for their employers and their colleagues.

These 30 questions will measure your level of compliance and help to determine your level of agreeableness. The questions are simple; use the table below to answer the following questions. Circle the number that represents your answer and then use your answers to check your score.

Note: Reversed means that answering 'agree' or 'strongly agree' to the question will result in a low score of that trait.

1	2	3	4	5
Strongly Disagree	Disagree	Neutral	Agree	Strongly Agree

1. I refuse to concede an argument. (Reversed)

1	2	3	4	5

2. I tend to withdraw from heated discussions.

1	2	3	4	5

3. I dislike confrontation.

1	2	3	4	5

4. Workers should be polite and obedient.

1	2	3	4	5

5. I make the people I work with feel at ease.

1	2	3	4	5

6. I rarely get irritated by others.

1	2	3	4	5

7. I don't mind doing what I am asked.

1	2	3	4	5

8. I do what I am told without hesitation.

1	2	3	4	5

9. I have a short fuse. (Reversed)

1	2	3	4	5

10. I am willing to help others.

1	2	3	4	5

11. Seldom, I get in an argument at work.

1	2	3	4	5

12. I prefer obedient people as opposed to carefree people.

1	2	3	4	5

13. I follow the rules.

1	2	3	4	5

14. If I don't agree with something, I won't do it. (Reversed)

1	2	3	4	5

15. I usually adapt my behaviour so I don't upset anyone.

1	2	3	4	5

16. Even if I am right, I tend to withdraw from the argument first.

1	2	3	4	5

17. When it comes to my opinions, I stand firm and assert my thoughts and ideas. (Reversed)

1	2	3	4	5

18. I am willing to assist others if they need my help.

1	2	3	4	5

19. It is important for people to change how they act in order to fit in.

1	2	3	4	5

20. I often change my mind if other people disagree.

1	2	3	4	5

21. I find it easy to follow instruction.

1	2	3	4	5

22. I don't express anger in order to avoid a heated atmosphere.

1	2	3	4	5

23. When I disagree, I voice my opinions. (Reversed)

1	2	3	4	5

24. I am always obedient.

1	2	3	4	5

25. I do what I am told, regardless if I disagree with it.

1	2	3	4	5

26. I find it difficult to correct people if they are mistaken.

1	2	3	4	5

27. I prefer being polite with someone as opposed to being direct.

1	2	3	4	5

28. I avoid telling the truth to avoid hurting other people's feelings.

1	2	3	4	5

29. I am a cooperative person.

1	2	3	4	5

30. The workplace is no place for aggressive and assertive behaviour.

1	2	3	4	5

Scoring System:

Circle the number that represents your chosen answer:

Note: *make sure you circle the opposite answer from your above answer for the Reversed answers*

1. (R) 1 2 3 4 5	**2.** 1 2 3 4 5	**3.** 1 2 3 4 5	**4.** 1 2 3 4 5	**5.** 1 2 3 4 5
6. 1 2 3 4 5	**7.** 1 2 3 4 5	**8.** 1 2 3 4 5	**9.** (R) 1 2 3 4 5	**10.** 1 2 3 4 5
11. 1 2 3 4 5	**12.** 1 2 3 4 5	**13.** 1 2 3 4 5	**14.** (R) 1 2 3 4 5	**15.** 1 2 3 4 5
16. 1 2 3 4 5	**17.** (R) 1 2 3 4 5	**18.** 1 2 3 4 5	**19.** 1 2 3 4 5	**20.** 1 2 3 4 5
21. 1 2 3 4 5	**22.** 1 2 3 4 5	**23.** (R) 1 2 3 4 5	**24.** 1 2 3 4 5	**25.** 1 2 3 4 5
26. 1 2 3 4 5	**27.** 1 2 3 4 5	**28.** 1 2 3 4 5	**29.** 1 2 3 4 5	**30.** 1 2 3 4 5

SCORE TOTAL:	1's =	....	LOW
SCORE TOTAL:	2's =	....	
SCORE TOTAL:	3's =	....	AVERAGE
SCORE TOTAL:	4's =	....	
SCORE TOTAL:	5's =	....	HIGH

Circle your highest score.

Understanding Your Scores:

Your results on the Compliance test will help determine your overall outcome for the trait of Agreeableness. Once you've added up how many questions you answered strongly disagree, disagree, neutral, agree and strongly agree; it will be a clear way of distinguishing if your score was high, average or low.

If you answered mostly 5's or 4's, your score is going to demonstrate an extremely high level of trust. If you answered mostly 1's or 2's, your score is going to be extremely low. If you scored mostly 3's, you should read the average column.

HIGH (mostly 5's or 4's)	If you scored mostly 5's on the compliance test, you are showing extremely high levels of compliance. Compliance is this idea of morality. You tend to withdraw from conflict and confrontations. You are able to work well alongside others and don't feel the need to manipulate or challenge the people you work with. Being compliant in the workforce ensures a comfortable and stable work environment. Employers don't have to worry about people who are not following the rules. Compliancy is a valuable trait within any profession. It demonstrates the importance of trust and cooperation and morality that allows people to work as efficiently as possible. However, you want to border the high and low boundaries. You do not want to come across as the type of person who cannot voice an opinion if a situation required, however you also do not want to come across as assertive and the type of person who can't follow order.
AVERAGE (mostly 3's)	If you scored an average mark in the compliance test, it means that your compliancy is about average. Compliancy is often linked to this idea of morals and respect. You are the type of person who does not feel the need to cause conflict or confrontation in the work place. You tend to stick to yourself and get on with your job. Employers like to see compliant workers because it guarantees that their employees will follow the rules, get their job done and cooperate with the working environment. However, sometimes a situation requires you to think outside the rules. You might come up with a better idea that others may not have thought of and therefore you need to be able to express that idea. Whilst you usually follow order, you sometimes go with your own ideas in belief of gaining a better result.

LOW (mostly 1's or 2's)	If you scored mostly 1's on the compliance test, you are showing extremely low levels of compliancy. Extreme low levels of compliance suggests that you are unable to follow suit. In other words, you lack the ability to follow instruction. Low scorers believe that a certain amount of deception and suspicion in social relationships is necessary. This is not to say that low scorers are immoral; they are simply more guarded and apprehensive. However, an extreme low score for compliancy is undesirable to employers. Any business seeking people for their workforce want to ensure stable and efficient employees. They want to be able to set tasks and give instruction with little argument and hesitation. So, you want to be above the borderline in terms of compliancy. Compliant people are the most valuable in any job profession. It guarantees maximum work potential and therefore you want to be able to demonstrate this through your personality test.

ALTRUISM

Another way in which agreeableness is measured is through this notion of Altruism. Altruism is the idea of concern for other people's welfare. This manifestation involves doing things simply out of desire to help, and not because you have to.

Everyday life is filled with small acts of altruistic behaviour. However, it is a desirable quality in terms of personality traits in which employer's value.

High scoring for altruistic behaviour demonstrates your ability to make people feel welcome and take an interest in the welfare of people around you. They are sympathetic to others and are willing to help them.

Low scorers of altruism show little interest in other people and therefore are often people who are concerned more so with themselves. These people tend to be more self-centred and reluctant of interfering with other people's wellbeing.

Employers want to be assured of a workforce that are willing to help others and demonstrate high levels of gratification, empathy and consideration. Being altruistic allows a clear understanding of the type of person you are and how well you get along with other people. It is important in the work place to not only think of yourself and your job prospects, but to also work alongside others and give help if someone asks.

These 30 questions will measure your level of altruism and help to determine your level of agreeableness. The questions are simple; use the table below to answer the following questions. Circle the number that represents your answer and then use your answers to check your score.

Note: Reversed means that answering 'agree' or 'strongly agree' to the question will result in a low score of that trait.

1	2	3	4	5
Strongly Disagree	Disagree	Neutral	Agree	Strongly Agree

1. I assist other people when I can.

1	2	3	4	5

2. Sometimes, people don't want your help, so I don't interfere. (Reversed)

1	2	3	4	5

3. I assist other people even at a personal cost.

1	2	3	4	5

4. I am always willing to help other people regardless.

1	2	3	4	5

5. I believe it is important to work as a team.

1	2	3	4	5

6. I would rather work on my own. (Reversed)

1	2	3	4	5

7. I usually adapt my behaviour so I work better with people.

1	2	3	4	5

8. I do my upmost to make people feel welcome.

1	2	3	4	5

9. I try and help others when I can.

1	2	3	4	5

10. I am usually the person who helps the new employee.

1	2	3	4	5

11. I make an effort to get to know everyone I work with.

1	2	3	4	5

12. I help others with their work before I work on my own.

1	2	3	4	5

13. I seldom judge people before I get to know them.

1	2	3	4	5

14. I have given a colleague a lift home from work.

1	2	3	4	5

15. I often open doors for other members of staff.

1	2	3	4	5

16. I always make the effort to greet everyone in the morning.

1	2	3	4	5

17. I have helped carry a colleagues belongings if they looked like they were overloaded.

1	2	3	4	5

18. I sometimes take some workload off a colleague if I feel they are struggling.

1	2	3	4	5

19. I think about myself before others. (Reversed)

1	2	3	4	5

20. I work best if I am working in a team.

1	2	3	4	5

21. I do my upmost to ensure a happy and comfortable atmosphere.

1	2	3	4	5

22. I always help others when I can.

1	2	3	4	5

23. I am reluctant to get involved with other people's welfare. (Reversed)

1	2	3	4	5

24. I consider myself a selfless person.

1	2	3	4	5

25. It is important for me to help others.

1	2	3	4	5

26. I help people because I want to, not because I have to.

1	2	3	4	5

27. I have assisted someone working towards a deadline.

1	2	3	4	5

28. I have retrieved an item dropped by one of my colleagues.

1	2	3	4	5

29. I have made changes in my workload to help others with theirs.

1	2	3	4	5

30. I consider myself an unselfish person.

1	2	3	4	5

Scoring System:

Circle the number that represents your chosen answer:

Note: make sure you circle the opposite answer from your above answer for the Reversed answers

1.	2.	3.	4.	5.
1 2 3 4 5	(R) 1 2 3 4 5	1 2 3 4 5	1 2 3 4 5	1 2 3 4 5
6.	7.	8.	9.	10.
(R) 1 2 3 4 5	1 2 3 4 5	1 2 3 4 5	1 2 3 4 5	1 2 3 4 5
11.	12.	13.	14.	15.
1 2 3 4 5	1 2 3 4 5	1 2 3 4 5	1 2 3 4 5	1 2 3 4 5
16.	17.	18.	19.	20.
1 2 3 4 5	1 2 3 4 5	1 2 3 4 5	(R) 1 2 3 4 5	1 2 3 4 5
21.	22.	23.	24.	25.
1 2 3 4 5	1 2 3 4 5	(R) 1 2 3 4 5	1 2 3 4 5	1 2 3 4 5
26.	27.	28.	29.	30.
1 2 3 4 5	1 2 3 4 5	1 2 3 4 5	1 2 3 4 5	1 2 3 4 5

SCORE TOTAL:	1's =	....	LOW
SCORE TOTAL:	2's =	....	
SCORE TOTAL:	3's =	....	AVERAGE
SCORE TOTAL:	4's =	....	
SCORE TOTAL:	5's =	....	HIGH

Circle your highest score.

Understanding Your Scores:

Your results on the Altruism test will help determine your overall outcome for the trait of Agreeableness. Once you've added up how many questions you answered strongly disagree, disagree, neutral, agree and strongly agree; it will be a clear way of distinguishing if your score was high, average or low.

If you answered mostly 5's or 4's, your score is going to demonstrate an extremely high level of trust. If you answered mostly 1's or 2's, your score is going to be extremely low. If you scored mostly 3's, you should read the average column.

HIGH (mostly 5's or 4's)	If you answered mostly 5's, it suggests your personality has an extremely high level of altruistic behaviour.

This means that you always think of others before yourself, you are empathetic towards your colleagues and will help them out whenever you can.

You are selfless, you are warm and soft-hearted and like to contribute to a calm and relaxed atmosphere.

You're the type of person who works well as part of a team. You do your work but you also help others with theirs.

High levels of altruism is a vital part of any business. A business desires a workforce who are capable of working alongside one another. Employers like to see employees helping out colleagues in order to get the work done.

However, being extremely altruistic may result in people taking advantage of you. You don't want to be doing other people's work just because they don't want to do it. You want to be able to show that you are willing to help if the situation requires it. |
| **AVERAGE (mostly 3's)** | If you answered mostly 3's in the altruistic test, it means that you scored an average score.

An average score indicates that you are empathetic and friendly to the people around you. You often consider other people's feelings and help them when you can.

However, if a situation requires you to think about yourself first, you are not afraid to do so. This may show levels of selfishness, but getting to where you want to be and achieving your goals is at the top of your list.

Whilst you're a team player and get on with other people, you often need to think about yourself in terms of where you're heading and the opportunities that may arise.

When the time comes, employers like to see not only people who are able to work alongside people, but are also the type are of people who are driven and willing to succeed. |

LOW (mostly 1's or 2's)	If you answered mostly 1's in the altruism test, this suggests that you have an extremely low level of altruism. Extreme low scores in the altruism test reinforces your lack of agreeableness. You're the type of person who thinks about themselves first. You get your work done and worry about your tasks and deadlines. You take no interest in interfering with other people's welfare. You look after yourself to keep ahead of the game and make sure you are on track. Although employers like to see employees who can work independently and get on with their job without any help; refusing to help others or refusing others to help you means that you cannot gain another perspective or pick up on something you may have missed. You want to be able to show to employers that you can work independently and in a team to ensure maximum business potential. Helping others shouldn't be something you feel you have to do, but something that you want to do in order to create a relaxed atmosphere and get the work done to the best standard.

TENDER-MINDEDNESS

The last facet of identifying a person's agreeableness is tender-mindedness. Tender-mindedness is a term used to describe people who show compassion, empathy and mercifulness. This trait indicates the extent to which a person shows a caring and helpful persona.

People who score highly on the tender-mindedness test usually show traits of compassion and sympathy and attentiveness towards other people's needs.

Low scores for this test shows their lack of affection towards human suffering. These people tend to be more concerned with truth and justice rather than with mercy. They show lack of sympathy towards others.

These 30 questions will measure your level of tender-mindedness and help to determine your level of agreeableness. The questions are simple; use the table below to answer the following questions. Circle the number that represents your answer and then use your answers to check your score.

Note: Reversed means that answering 'agree' or 'strongly agree' to the question will result in a low score of that trait.

1	2	3	4	5
Strongly Disagree	Disagree	Neutral	Agree	Strongly Agree

1. I believe that all people, without exception, are entitled to human dignity.

1	2	3	4	5

2. Everyone deserves respect.

1	2	3	4	5

3. I consider myself a compassionate person.

1	2	3	4	5

4. You can't judge a book by its cover.

1	2	3	4	5

5. I consider myself a sympathetic person.

1	2	3	4	5

6. I would rather be considered a sympathetic person as opposed to a person with strong morals.

1	2	3	4	5

7. I feel empathetic to people less fortunate than myself.

1	2	3	4	5

8. I'm always merciful

1	2	3	4	5

9. Everyone should be treated equally.

1	2	3	4	5

10. Our fate is in our own hands.

1	2	3	4	5

11. I feel useless when I meet someone less fortunate than myself.

1	2	3	4	5

12. I don't worry about other people's wellbeing. (Reversed)

1	2	3	4	5

13. You have to look after number one. (Reversed)

1	2	3	4	5

14. We all need to help and respect one another.

1	2	3	4	5

15. We live in an unfair world.

1	2	3	4	5

16. I seldom think I am superior.

1	2	3	4	5

17. I never think I am better than anyone else.

1	2	3	4	5

18. I am extremely empathetic.

1	2	3	4	5

19. I admire people who don't have much but are content with who they are.

1	2	3	4	5

20. Sometimes I stop to think about what people are going through.

1	2	3	4	5

21. I am more concerned with the truth and justice rather than mercy. (reversed)

1	2	3	4	5

22. I do my part in the community and help the elderly.

1	2	3	4	5

23. I often judge a person before getting to know them. (Reversed)

1	2	3	4	5

24. I always look for the best in others.

1	2	3	4	5

25. I have a traditional sense of morality.

1	2	3	4	5

26. I feel little concern for others. (Reversed)

1	2	3	4	5

27. I put the needs of others ahead of my own.

1	2	3	4	5

28. We all need a little help every once in a while.

1	2	3	4	5

29. I consider myself a selfless person.

1	2	3	4	5

30. I don't care for people who think they're above everybody else.

1	2	3	4	5

Scoring System:

Circle the number that represents your chosen answer:

Note: make sure you circle the opposite answer from your above answer for the Reversed answers

1.	2.	3.	4.	5.
1 2 3 4 5	1 2 3 4 5	1 2 3 4 5	1 2 3 4 5	1 2 3 4 5
6.	**7.**	**8.**	**9.**	**10.**
1 2 3 4 5	1 2 3 4 5	1 2 3 4 5	1 2 3 4 5	1 2 3 4 5
11.	**12.** (R)	**13.** (R)	**14.**	**15.**
1 2 3 4 5	1 2 3 4 5	1 2 3 4 5	1 2 3 4 5	1 2 3 4 5
16.	**17.**	**18.**	**19.**	**20.**
1 2 3 4 5	1 2 3 4 5	1 2 3 4 5	1 2 3 4 5	1 2 3 4 5
21. (R)	**22.**	**23.** (R)	**24.**	**25.**
1 2 3 4 5	1 2 3 4 5	1 2 3 4 5	1 2 3 4 5	1 2 3 4 5
26. (R)	**27.**	**28.**	**29.**	**30.**
1 2 3 4 5	1 2 3 4 5	1 2 3 4 5	1 2 3 4 5	1 2 3 4 5

SCORE TOTAL:	1's =	....	LOW
SCORE TOTAL:	2's =	....	
SCORE TOTAL:	3's =	....	AVERAGE
SCORE TOTAL:	4's =	....	
SCORE TOTAL:	5's =	....	HIGH

Circle your highest score.

Understanding Your Scores:

Your results on the Tender-mindedness test will help determine your overall outcome for the trait of Agreeableness. Once you've added up how many questions you answered strongly disagree, disagree, neutral, agree and strongly agree; it will be a clear way of distinguishing if your score was high, average or low.

If you answered mostly 5's or 4's, your score is going to demonstrate an extremely high level of trust. If you answered mostly 1's or 2's, your score is going to be extremely low. If you scored mostly 3's, you should read the average column.

HIGH (mostly 5's or 4's)	If you score mostly 5's, it suggests that you maintain an extreme high level of tender-mindedness. Extreme high levels of tender-mindedness suggests a great deal of empathy and compassion. You are a considerate and caring person. You value the importance of helping others and will often help others needs before your own. You tend to understand what people are going through and how they may be feeling and you can provide a caring and sympathetic approach. Extreme high levels can be seen as a disadvantage. Whilst being compassionate and empathetic is great, showing extreme levels may suggest to employers that the person is too compassionate, too involved and showing lack of rationale and composure.
AVERAGE (mostly 3's)	If you scored mostly 3's, this means that you show an average score of tender-mindedness. You are the type of person who shows empathy and compassion towards the people around you. You like to help others when you can and provide a sympathetic attitude towards them. Sometimes you feel as though it is not your place to get involved and therefore show a more reserved approach. Some people don't want others to get involved, and therefore you don't want to get in the way where you are not wanted. Although you are concerned with the welfare of other people, you also think truth and justice is important too. This is where you show other levels of tender-mindedness. You sometimes show little compassion towards other people. You may find it difficult to separate the truth from empathy.

LOW (mostly 1's or 2's)	If you score mostly 1's in the tender-mindedness, it means that you show extreme low levels of compassion and empathy. These people tend to be more self-centred and reserved. They don't take any interest in other people's wellbeing and focus on themselves. Low scorers are more concerned with truth and justice rather than morality and sympathy. They show lack of affection towards human suffering and therefore show little compassion. Employers do not like people having the trait that shows lack of affection and sympathy. They want employees to show that they care and take consideration into subject matters. They want to ensure people are rational and composed, whilst demonstrating certain aspects of tender-mindedness.

How Agreeable Are You?

So, you've finished answering all the questions on Agreeableness. We have provided the table below to generate a general understanding of your level of agreeableness.

Now go back through the six sub-traits for Agreeableness and use your high, average and low scores to fill in the table below.

TRAIT	Trust	Straight-forwardness	Altruism	Compli-ance	Modesty	Tender - Mindedness
HIGH, AVERAGE OR LOW?						

What does this mean overall?

HIGH	Agreeableness is primarily a dimension to measure a person's interpersonal tendencies. People who score highly over the Agreeableness chapter, will show high levels of trust and compliance and other contributing factors assessed throughout the chapter. You are the type of person who carries the traits of sympathy and cooperative. You are considered friendly, empathetic and generally kind hearted. Depending on your occupation, it depends how agreeable you should be. In the following chapter, you will be able to assess your traits in recognition to your job role and how this proves either beneficial or undesirable. Agreeableness reflects how well an individual can get along with other people and how they react in social situations. They have an optimistic view of human nature and therefore believe in honesty, trustworthiness and common decency. **TRAITS = trusting, soft-hearted, sympathetic, generous, altruistic, cooperative**

AVERAGE	If you scored an average score for most of the sub-traits of agreeableness, this indicates that you have shown both levels of high and low scoring attributes. Overall, you are a kind-hearted, warm, and sympathetic person who generally gets along with most people. Although you may find it difficult to like everyone, you often take it in your stride. You are considered an agreeable person. You follow the rules, you get along with people and you tend to take instruction well. However, sometimes you like to voice your opinion and therefore cause some level of disagreeableness. Employers like to see that people are able to disagree with something if the situation requires it and is in the best interest overall. **TRAITS = attentive, sympathetic, cooperative, independent, confident, assertive**
LOW	If you scored low in most of the sub-traits of agreeableness, this suggests that you place self-interest above helping others. Low scorers are often sceptical and suspicious about other people. You tend to be unfriendly and withdrawn from social situations due to lack of trust and reliance on other people. You are assertive and demanding. You like to view your opinions and make sure your voice is heard. You are not afraid to confront other people and you not afraid of creating confrontation or dispute. You tend to be quite shrewd and perceptive. Your pessimistic and antagonistic attitude suggests you find it difficult to maintain a stable and comfortable work ethic. People who score a low often find it best to work independently as opposed to working in a team. You don't like to interact or engage with social interactivity and find it difficult to show cooperation, trust and empathy towards others. **TRAITS = sceptical, suspicious, pessimistic, hard-hearted, demanding, assertive, antagonistic**

What does this say to employers about your personality?

A person who is willing to show cooperation, morality and agreeableness is a person that employers value. They like to see people are able to work as a team, trust the others they work with and maintain a balanced and happy work environment.

You want to be able to show a balance between agreeing and cooperating with work colleagues and being able to demonstrate independent thinking and initiative when required. Scoring above average for this test shows the potential for a strong candidate who has the desirable qualities needed for the job role.

CHAPTER 3 - The Big 5:

Extroversion

CHAPTER 3 - THE BIG 5: EXTROVERSION

The Big 5 model of personality argues that every personality can be understood by looking at five personality traits. Extroversion is a term that most people are familiar with. Used alongside introversion, it measures a person's ability to engage with their social surroundings and how adaptable they are in social relationships.

Extroversion can be defined as the extent to which a person is 'sociable'. In broad terms, they tend to be people who are people-orientated and enjoy engaging in social relationships. In addition, they are outgoing, dynamic and have a need for companionship. They show an optimistic attitude and seek the excitement and stimulation of cheerful dispositions and being a part of something 'social'.

Unlike introverts, extroverts like to be talkative and active. They like to feel like part of a crowd. They are often assertive. They are the type of people who usually say 'yes' or 'let's go' and relish in the thoughts of excitement and opportunity.

Whereas, introverts tend to be withdrawn and reserved. They lack exuberance and energy. They're often quiet and disengaged from the social world and prefer not to be interrupted.

There are several sub-traits that personality tests look at to measure extroversion. These indicate your engagements of the 'social' world which are often analysed in terms of **warmth, gregariousness, assertiveness, excitement seeking, positive emotions and activity.**

In this chapter, it will focus on each one of these terms and assess your personality to determine your level of extroversion.

WARMTH

One of the facets of Extroversion is this notion of warmth. People who provide warmth have the tendency to show levels of friendliness and affection. They show a genuine interest in others and demonstrate positive feelings towards others. They make friends easily and enjoy the company of others.

People who score highly regarding warmth and friendliness are those people who enjoy other peoples company and show a general regard for others.

Low scorers are people who are somewhat more formal and distant. They are reserved in their approach with others and tend to hold back from becoming 'too' friendly.

These 30 questions will measure your level of warmth and friendliness to help to determine your level of extroversion. The questions are simple; use the table below to answer the following questions. Circle the number that represents your answer and then use your answers to check your score.

Note: Reversed means that answering 'agree' or 'strongly agree' to the question will result in a low score of that trait.

1	2	3	4	5
Strongly Disagree	Disagree	Neutral	Agree	Strongly Agree

1. I make friends easily.

1	2	3	4	5

2. I consider myself a talkative person.

1	2	3	4	5

3. I like going to social gatherings.

1	2	3	4	5

4. I feel at ease when I am around lots of people.

1	2	3	4	5

5. Starting a conversation is easy for me.

1	2	3	4	5

6. I make the effort to start a conversation.

1	2	3	4	5

7. I am better at talking than listening.

1	2	3	4	5

8. I consider myself an outgoing person.

1	2	3	4	5

9. I rarely feel blue.

1	2	3	4	5

10. I enjoy having lots of people around me.

1	2	3	4	5

11. I seldom feel overwhelmed by large crowds.

1	2	3	4	5

12. I reach out to others when I can.

1	2	3	4	5

13. I have positive attitudes towards other people.

1	2	3	4	5

14. I am not hostile towards other people.

1	2	3	4	5

15. I am quick at making new friends.

1	2	3	4	5

16. I often start conversations.

1	2	3	4	5

17. I have little to say. (Reversed)

1	2	3	4	5

18. I often like being the centre of attention.

1	2	3	4	5

19. I make people feel at ease.

1	2	3	4	5

20. I do my upmost to welcome new people.

1	2	3	4	5

21. I consider myself a sociable person.

1	2	3	4	5

22. I am upbeat and optimistic.

1	2	3	4	5

23. I like to be independent (Reversed).

1	2	3	4	5

24. I find it easy to form close relationships.

1	2	3	4	5

25. I am reserved and shy. (Reversed)

1	2	3	4	5

26. Sometimes, I come across as over friendly.

1	2	3	4	5

27. I am easy to get to know as a person.

1	2	3	4	5

28. I have often been told I am too considerate.

1	2	3	4	5

29. I like people.

1	2	3	4	5

30. I prefer being on my own. (Reversed)

1	2	3	4	5

Scoring System:

Circle the number that represents your chosen answer:

Note: make sure you circle the opposite answer from your above answer for the Reversed answers

1.	2.	3.	4.	5.
1 2 3 4 5	1 2 3 4 5	1 2 3 4 5	1 2 3 4 5	1 2 3 4 5
6.	7.	8.	9.	10.
1 2 3 4 5	1 2 3 4 5	1 2 3 4 5	1 2 3 4 5	1 2 3 4 5
11.	12.	13.	14.	15.
1 2 3 4 5	1 2 3 4 5	1 2 3 4 5	1 2 3 4 5	1 2 3 4 5
16.	17.	18.	19.	20.
1 2 3 4 5	(R) 1 2 3 4 5	1 2 3 4 5	1 2 3 4 5	1 2 3 4 5
21.	22.	23.	24.	25.
1 2 3 4 5	1 2 3 4 5	(R) 1 2 3 4 5	1 2 3 4 5	(R) 1 2 3 4 5
26.	27.	28.	29.	30.
1 2 3 4 5	1 2 3 4 5	1 2 3 4 5	1 2 3 4 5	(R) 1 2 3 4 5

SCORE TOTAL:	1's =	....	LOW
SCORE TOTAL:	2's =	....	
SCORE TOTAL:	3's =	....	AVERAGE
SCORE TOTAL:	4's =	....	
SCORE TOTAL:	5's =	....	HIGH

Circle your highest score.

Understanding Your Scores:

Your results on the Warmth and friendliness test will help determine your overall outcome for the trait of Extroversion. Once you've added up how many questions you answered strongly disagree, disagree, neutral, agree and strongly agree; it will be a clear way of distinguishing if your score was high, average or low.

If you answered mostly 5's or 4's, your score is going to demonstrate an extremely high level of trust. If you answered mostly 1's or 2's, your score is going to be extremely low. If you scored mostly 3's, you should read the average column.

HIGH (mostly 5's or 4's)	If you scored mostly 5's, it means you have an extremely high warmth attribute. High scorers for the facet of warmth reinforces your friendly approach towards others. You have a genuine interest in the wellbeing of other people and you enjoy getting to know them. You are a kind, caring and considerate person who finds it easy to make new friends and start a conversation with someone. Your personality shines through as being upbeat, outgoing and dynamic. You are comfortable in social gatherings and enjoy the stimulation and excitement from others. Employers like to know that their employees are people who most people will be able to get along with and work with in a relaxed atmosphere. Being friendly demonstrates your ability to get along with others and make an effort to engage with the people around you.
AVERAGE (mostly 3's)	An average score of warmth and friendliness demonstrates social engagement and ability to work as a team as well as being independent and reserved. An average score means that you are generally considered a kind, caring and considerate person who gets along with people. You are comfortable in social situations and enjoy being in a dynamic atmosphere. However, you also show traits of reservation and independence which you also value. Whilst you do enjoy being in the company of others, you are not afraid to be on your own and distance yourself from the crowd. Sometimes you come across as shy and timid. You may find it difficult to come up with new conversations and therefore feel guarded in terms of what you say or do.

LOW (mostly 1's or 2's)	If you scored mostly 1's, it suggests that you're the type of person who finds it difficult to be friendly with others. Low scorers are often people that tend to be reserved. They are shy and distant and make it difficult for others to get to know them. Therefore, it makes them difficult to approach and start a conversation with. Whilst these are people who score lowly on warmth and friendliness, it does not mean to say that they are cold and hostile towards others. They are simply more aloof and guarded and tend to stick by themselves. However, it makes it hard for people to approach you and therefore being considered cold and hostile might be how people perceive you. You need to be able to engage with social activity. Employers like to see 'team players'.

GREGARIOUSNESS

In order to assess one's behaviour and determine if they are extroverted or introverted, the term gregariousness is also assessed. Gregariousness is similar to the previous term warmth. It measures a person's ability to show that they are outgoing, sociable and fond of others.

A person who scores highly for gregariousness, demonstrates the above attributes – outgoing and dynamic. It is their preference to be in the company of others as opposed to being on their own. They like large crowds and like to feel that they are part of something big! They enjoy social engagements and need the stimulation they feel when being around other people.

Low scorers are people who are much more withdrawn from social situations. They have a tendency to feel overwhelmed by people and therefore avoid large parties and social gatherings. People who score a low score for this test are not necessarily people who don't like people. They are people who prefer to be in their own company and value their privacy more.

These 30 questions will measure your level of gregariousness to help to determine your level of extroversion. The questions are simple; use the table below to answer the following questions. Circle the number that represents your answer and then use your answers to check your score.

Note: Reversed means that answering 'agree' or 'strongly agree' to the question will result in a low score of that trait.

1	2	3	4	5
Strongly Disagree	Disagree	Neutral	Agree	Strongly Agree

1. I enjoy being part of a large crowd.

1	2	3	4	5

2. I enjoy being in the company of others.

1	2	3	4	5

3. I feel the need for social stimulation.

1	2	3	4	5

4. I like to be on my own. (Reversed)

1	2	3	4	5

5. I like to feel part of a group.

1	2	3	4	5

6. I am always with people.

1	2	3	4	5

7. I make friends easily.

1	2	3	4	5

8. I find it easy to talk to someone I don't know.

1	2	3	4	5

9. I find it easy to fit in amongst people.

1	2	3	4	5

10. I believe it is important to engage in social activity.

1	2	3	4	5

11. I would rather go out with friends then be stuck indoors on my own.

1	2	3	4	5

12. Seldom, you will find me on my own.

1	2	3	4	5

13. I feel like I do things more so on my own. (Reversed)

1	2	3	4	5

14. I like to follow the crowd.

1	2	3	4	5

15. I am comfortable in most social situations.

1	2	3	4	5

16. I like to feel like I belong in a group.

1	2	3	4	5

17. The best part of my day is when I am on my own. (Reversed)

1	2	3	4	5

18. Any chance of a large party and I am there.

| 1 | 2 | 3 | 4 | 5 |

19. I often find myself surrounded by lots of people.

| 1 | 2 | 3 | 4 | 5 |

20. I avoid social gatherings. (Reversed)

| 1 | 2 | 3 | 4 | 5 |

21. Companionship is important to me.

| 1 | 2 | 3 | 4 | 5 |

22. I value social excitement more than my privacy.

| 1 | 2 | 3 | 4 | 5 |

23. I consider myself an outgoing and dynamic person.

| 1 | 2 | 3 | 4 | 5 |

24. I value my time more when I am with others.

| 1 | 2 | 3 | 4 | 5 |

25. If all my friends go out, I have to go too.

| 1 | 2 | 3 | 4 | 5 |

26. I hate being on my own.

| 1 | 2 | 3 | 4 | 5 |

27. I enjoy a dynamic environment packed full of people.

| 1 | 2 | 3 | 4 | 5 |

28. I consider myself a sociable person.

| 1 | 2 | 3 | 4 | 5 |

29. I am more extroverted than introverted.

| 1 | 2 | 3 | 4 | 5 |

30. It is important to feel like you are part of something 'big' and 'exciting'.

| 1 | 2 | 3 | 4 | 5 |

Scoring System:

Circle the number that represents your chosen answer:

Note: make sure you circle the opposite answer from your above answer for the Reversed answers

1.		2.		3.		4.		5.	
	1 2 3 4 5		1 2 3 4 5		1 2 3 4 5	(R)	1 2 3 4 5		1 2 3 4 5
6.		7.		8.		9.		10.	
	1 2 3 4 5		1 2 3 4 5		1 2 3 4 5		1 2 3 4 5		1 2 3 4 5
11.		12.		13.		14.		15.	
	1 2 3 4 5		1 2 3 4 5	(R)	1 2 3 4 5		1 2 3 4 5		1 2 3 4 5
16.		17.		18.		19.		20.	
	1 2 3 4 5	(R)	1 2 3 4 5		1 2 3 4 5		1 2 3 4 5	(R)	1 2 3 4 5
21.		22.		23.		24.		25.	
	1 2 3 4 5		1 2 3 4 5		1 2 3 4 5		1 2 3 4 5		1 2 3 4 5
26.		27.		28.		29.		30.	
	1 2 3 4 5		1 2 3 4 5		1 2 3 4 5		1 2 3 4 5		1 2 3 4 5

SCORE TOTAL:	1's =	....	LOW
SCORE TOTAL:	2's =	....	
SCORE TOTAL:	3's =	....	AVERAGE
SCORE TOTAL:	4's =	....	
SCORE TOTAL:	5's =	....	HIGH

Circle your highest score.

Understanding Your Scores:

Your results on the gregariousness test will help determine your overall outcome for the trait of Extroversion. Once you've added up how many questions you answered strongly disagree, disagree, neutral, agree and strongly agree; it will be a clear way of distinguishing if your score was high, average or low.

If you answered mostly 5's or 4's, your score is going to demonstrate an extremely high level of trust. If you answered mostly 1's or 2's, your score is going to be extremely low. If you scored mostly 3's, you should read the average column.

HIGH (mostly 5's or 4's)	Scoring highly on this scale means that you are extremely gregarious. Gregarious is a term usually used to describe a person who is sociably outgoing, enthusiastic and dynamic. You revel in opportunities that place you in large crowds or social gatherings. You prefer the company of others as opposed to being on your own. High gregariousness indicates an extrovert's need for companionship. If you are applying for a job where you will be spending most of your time on your own, you don't want to come across as a person who really needs to be around people. Therefore, depending on the role you are applying for, depends whereabouts on the scale you want to score. So, make sure you know what traits are desirable for your chosen job role and see if your traits match the expectations.
AVERAGE (mostly 3's)	If you scored an average score on the scale for gregariousness, it means that your personality shows both characteristics of independence and socialness. You do not mind whether you are left on your own to your own devices or in a large crowd. You feel comfortable in either situation and therefore demonstrate adaptability and versatility. You enjoy going out socially and engaging in a dynamic and outgoing atmosphere but you also like your privacy and appreciate the time you get to have by yourself. Depending on the job role you are applying for, depends how much gregariousness you want to demonstrate. But an average score shows that you are more adaptable in a variety of social situations and therefore employers will admire that. You need to demonstrate both levels of independence and control as well as being a team player and socially engaging.

LOW (mostly 1's or 2's)	If you score a low score on the scale of gregariousness, it means that your persona comes across as more independent.

You prefer to be on your own. You avoid large parties and social gatherings because you feel shy, awkward and uncomfortable.

You value your privacy more than going out with a group of people. You value your time on your own and don't feel the need to be constantly with groups of people.

Low scorers of gregariousness are much more introverted. You tend to be more withdrawn and reserved. This doesn't mean to say that low scorers don't like people, it just means that you feel more comfortable and satisfied in your own company.

If you are applying for a job which is very people orientated and will require you to be in large groups of people, you want to aim for a slightly more average score on the scale. You do not want to come across as solely independent; employers need to be ensured that you are capable of working in large groups and feel comfortable in doing so (because people will be able to notice from your behaviour and body language if you are feeling uncomfortable!) |

ASSERTIVENESS

Measuring a person's assertiveness is another way to assess a person's overall extroversion. The term assertiveness refers to a person's ability to take charge. It is the quality of being self-assured and confident without being aggressive or hostile. It is a form of behaviour that can be characterised by affirmation and the ability to give direction and speak out.

People who score highly on this scale show great levels of confidence and self-assurance and are able to put across their views and opinions in a direct manner. They are people who are not afraid to stand up for themselves and speak their mind. They tend to be the leaders of groups. They are able to give good direction and instruction to others and form a constructive take-charge approach.

Low scorers of assertiveness are those people who prefer to be less active. They take a more relaxed approach and allow other people to take charge. They tend not to be the leaders of the groups due to lack of self-assurance and confidence to speak out and take control.

These 30 questions will measure your level of assertiveness to help to determine your level of extroversion. The questions are simple; use the table below to answer the following questions. Circle the number that represents your answer and then use your answers to check your score.

__Note: Reversed means that answering 'agree' or 'strongly agree' to the question will result in a low score of that trait.__

1	2	3	4	5
Strongly Disagree	Disagree	Neutral	Agree	Strongly Agree

1.   I deal with difficult situations.

1	2	3	4	5

2.   I voice my opinions.

1	2	3	4	5

3.   I am a self-confident person.

1	2	3	4	5

4.   I am often the leader of the group.

1	2	3	4	5

5. I take charge.

1	2	3	4	5

6. I feel free to politely give my thoughts on a situation.

1	2	3	4	5

7. I am often considered easy going (Reversed)

1	2	3	4	5

8. I enjoy taking control of difficult situations.

1	2	3	4	5

9. I am good at leading people.

1	2	3	4	5

10. I am never the leader amongst a group of people. (Reversed)

1	2	3	4	5

11. I am a confident person.

1	2	3	4	5

12. I believe I have the skills to lead a group.

1	2	3	4	5

13. I feel comfortable saying no to people.

1	2	3	4	5

14. It is important to be able to express your concerns and thoughts about something.

1	2	3	4	5

15. I take charge and tackle the problem on my own.

1	2	3	4	5

16. I tend to just go along with what everyone is doing. (Reversed)

1	2	3	4	5

17. I am a laid back person. (Reversed)

1	2	3	4	5

18. Sometimes I intimidate people to get something done.

| 1 | 2 | 3 | 4 | 5 |

19. I am often firm when dealing with others.

| 1 | 2 | 3 | 4 | 5 |

20. Most people around me seem more assertive than I am. (Reversed)

| 1 | 2 | 3 | 4 | 5 |

21. If there is a problem, it is usually me who will deal with it.

| 1 | 2 | 3 | 4 | 5 |

22. I believe it is important to be able to manage a team.

| 1 | 2 | 3 | 4 | 5 |

23. I manage a team effectively and successfully.

| 1 | 2 | 3 | 4 | 5 |

24. I like being the centre of attention.

| 1 | 2 | 3 | 4 | 5 |

25. I tend to blend myself in with others in order to not be noticed. (Reversed)

| 1 | 2 | 3 | 4 | 5 |

26. I am able to express my needs and feelings rationally and firmly.

| 1 | 2 | 3 | 4 | 5 |

27. I find it easy to say what I want.

| 1 | 2 | 3 | 4 | 5 |

28. I can take full responsibility of my own feelings and behaviours.

| 1 | 2 | 3 | 4 | 5 |

29. I am firm and direct.

| 1 | 2 | 3 | 4 | 5 |

30. It annoys me when people don't say what they really mean.

| 1 | 2 | 3 | 4 | 5 |

Scoring System:

Circle the number that represents your chosen answer:

Note: make sure you circle the opposite answer from your above answer for the Reversed answers

1.	2.	3.	4.	5.
1 2 3 4 5	1 2 3 4 5	1 2 3 4 5	1 2 3 4 5	1 2 3 4 5
6.	**7.**	**8.**	**9.**	**10.**
1 2 3 4 5	*(R)* 1 2 3 4 5	1 2 3 4 5	1 2 3 4 5	*(R)* 1 2 3 4 5
11.	**12.**	**13.**	**14.**	**15.**
1 2 3 4 5	1 2 3 4 5	1 2 3 4 5	1 2 3 4 5	1 2 3 4 5
16.	**17.**	**18.**	**19.**	**20.**
(R) 1 2 3 4 5	*(R)* 1 2 3 4 5	1 2 3 4 5	1 2 3 4 5	*(R)* 1 2 3 4 5
21.	**22.**	**23.**	**24.**	**25.**
1 2 3 4 5	1 2 3 4 5	1 2 3 4 5	1 2 3 4 5	*(R)* 1 2 3 4 5
26.	**27.**	**28.**	**29.**	**30.**
1 2 3 4 5	1 2 3 4 5	1 2 3 4 5	1 2 3 4 5	1 2 3 4 5

SCORE TOTAL:	1's =	....	LOW
SCORE TOTAL:	2's =	....	
SCORE TOTAL:	3's =	....	AVERAGE
SCORE TOTAL:	4's =	....	
SCORE TOTAL:	5's =	....	HIGH

Circle your highest score.

Understanding Your Scores:

Your results on the assertiveness test will help determine your overall outcome for the trait of Extroversion. Once you've added up how many questions you answered strongly disagree, disagree, neutral, agree and strongly agree; it will be a clear way of distinguishing if your score was high, average or low.

If you answered mostly 5's or 4's, your score is going to demonstrate an extremely high level of trust. If you answered mostly 1's or 2's, your score is going to be extremely low. If you scored mostly 3's, you should read the average column.

HIGH (mostly 5's or 4's)	If you scored mostly 5's on the scale of the assertiveness test, it means you are extremely assertive. You have the ability to stand your own ground. You are confident and self-assured and are not afraid to say what you feel. You are able to take charge of a situation no matter how difficult or strenuous it may seem. You are able to think on your feet and come up with ideas of how to resolve something or what to do next. You are able to give direction. You are able to lead a team and give instruction. You have no fear of using the word "no", and you are not afraid to tell them what you think or want. Assertive people are people that are firm and direct but take into consideration the people around them. You are sensitive to subject matters when necessary and know what to say at the right time. Whilst being assertive reinforces your ability to take control of a situation, be the leader of a team and express your independent thinking; you don't want to score excessively on the test. Scoring excessively on the scale of assertiveness may come across as arrogant, egotistical and overconfident.
AVERAGE (mostly 3's)	An average score of assertiveness means that you are capable of showing firm and assertive decisions as well as demonstrating your ability to hold back. You are not afraid to stand your own ground when the situation requires you to do so. You are capable of taking charge if necessary and maintaining a group of people. You give direction and are able to lead a team. However, although you may be able to show assertiveness, you may not want that responsibility or may not enjoy the tasks of leading other people. You are more than happy to let someone else take the lead, but are able to step in if they need you.

**LOW
(mostly
1's or 2's)**

If you scored mostly 1's on the scale of the assertiveness test, it means you lack the assertive ability to express yourself.

Low scorers on the assertiveness test are people who wait for others to take the lead. They don't volunteer to take charge and they dislike the idea of being in control of a situation.

You are the type of person who is easy going and laid back. You don't mind doing what is asked of you but you don't like the thought of being the person that does the telling.

People who are less assertive are often considered shy and lack self-confidence. You don't have the ability to stand up in front of people and take charge. You are the type of person that often blends in with everyone else and prefers not to go noticed.

People who score extremely low on the assertive test should try to aim for an average score on the scale. Lack of assertiveness suggests you're incapable of expressing your thoughts and ideas.

Depending on your job role, you need to show some levels of assertiveness. You need to be able to show that you can think for yourself and express your ideas to other people. You don't want to place yourself as 'inferior' to everyone else – show your interest and speak out occasionally. Being assertive will help you gain confidence and the ability to stand out every once in a while.

EXCITEMENT-SEEKING

Another facet of Extroversion is the idea of excitement-seeking. In reference to job roles and how it is assessed within the work environment, excitement-seeking can refer to the people who seek stimulation and excitement. Excitement-seeking is a term that can be explored by assessing the extent to which a person seeks thrills and risks.

High scores for excitement-seekers are easily bored. They are people who relish in high levels of stimulation and keep things exhilarating. They show great levels of enthusiasm and eagerness to seek out risks and possible opportunities. They are not afraid to 'live on the edge'.

People who score low on the scale of excitement-seeking are adverse to thrill-seeking. They are people who prefer stability and familiarity. They do not like to seek adventure or risk; it makes them feel uncomfortable, nervous and overwhelmed. They tend to be people who like routine and structure.

These 30 questions will measure your level of excitement-seeking to help to determine your level of extroversion. The questions are simple; use the table below to answer the following questions. Circle the number that represents your answer and then use your answers to check your score.

Note: Reversed means that answering 'agree' or 'strongly agree' to the question will result in a low score of that trait.

1	2	3	4	5
Strongly Disagree	Disagree	Neutral	Agree	Strongly Agree

1. I often feel that I need to do something exciting.

1	2	3	4	5

2. I consider myself adventurous.

1	2	3	4	5

3. What is life without a little risk?

1	2	3	4	5

4. I prefer stability. (Reversed)

1	2	3	4	5

5. I would quit my current job if I got an interview for my perfect job.

1	2	3	4	5

6. I am not a cautious person.

1	2	3	4	5

7. A job that is familiar makes me feel secure and confident. (Reversed)

1	2	3	4	5

8. I always take risks.

1	2	3	4	5

9. I often 'do' before I 'think'.

1	2	3	4	5

10. I am constantly seeking excitement.

1	2	3	4	5

11. I find routine boring.

1	2	3	4	5

12. Most people would describe me as a risk-taker.

1	2	3	4	5

13. You have to take chances.

1	2	3	4	5

14. You won't know until you try.

1	2	3	4	5

15. I think about my actions carefully, I don't just do them. (Reversed)

1	2	3	4	5

16. I love taking risks.

1	2	3	4	5

17. Opportunities are rare; you have to take them whenever you can.

1	2	3	4	5

18. I am easily bored.

1	2	3	4	5

19. I live on the edge.

1	2	3	4	5

20. I get caught up in the moment.

1	2	3	4	5

21. Ambition and risk are important to me.

1	2	3	4	5

22. Sometimes I take risks to get one step closer.

1	2	3	4	5

23. You'll get nowhere in life if you don't take a risk every now and then.

1	2	3	4	5

24. I have previously put my career in jeopardy.

1	2	3	4	5

25. I have almost lost my job due to being too risky.

1	2	3	4	5

26. I consider myself a motivated and eager person who is willing to do anything it takes to succeed.

1	2	3	4	5

27. I like structure. (Reversed)

1	2	3	4	5

28. Sometimes, I like not knowing what comes next.

1	2	3	4	5

29. I am a thrill-seeker.

1	2	3	4	5

30. I take risks all the time so long as it doesn't hurt anyone else.

1	2	3	4	5

Scoring System:

Circle the number that represents your chosen answer:

Note: make sure you circle the opposite answer from your above answer for the Reversed answers

1. 1 2 3 4 5	**2.** 1 2 3 4 5	**3.** 1 2 3 4 5	**4.** *(R)* 1 2 3 4 5	**5.** 1 2 3 4 5
6. 1 2 3 4 5	**7.** *(R)* 1 2 3 4 5	**8.** 1 2 3 4 5	**9.** 1 2 3 4 5	**10.** 1 2 3 4 5
11. 1 2 3 4 5	**12.** 1 2 3 4 5	**13.** 1 2 3 4 5	**14.** 1 2 3 4 5	**15.** *(R)* 1 2 3 4 5
16. 1 2 3 4 5	**17.** 1 2 3 4 5	**18.** 1 2 3 4 5	**19.** 1 2 3 4 5	**20.** 1 2 3 4 5
21. 1 2 3 4 5	**22.** 1 2 3 4 5	**23.** 1 2 3 4 5	**24.** 1 2 3 4 5	**25.** 1 2 3 4 5
26. 1 2 3 4 5	**27.** *(R)* 1 2 3 4 5	**28.** 1 2 3 4 5	**29.** 1 2 3 4 5	**30.** 1 2 3 4 5

SCORE TOTAL:	1's =	....	LOW
SCORE TOTAL:	2's =	....	
SCORE TOTAL:	3's =	....	AVERAGE
SCORE TOTAL:	4's =	....	
SCORE TOTAL:	5's =	....	HIGH

Circle your highest score.

Understanding Your Scores:

Your results on the excitement-seeking test will help determine your overall outcome for the trait of Extroversion. Once you've added up how many questions you answered strongly disagree, disagree, neutral, agree and strongly agree; it will be a clear way of distinguishing if your score was high, average or low.

If you answered mostly 5's or 4's, your score is going to demonstrate an extremely high level of trust. If you answered mostly 1's or 2's, your score is going to be extremely low. If you scored mostly 3's, you should read the average column.

HIGH (mostly 5's or 4's)	If you scored mostly 5's on the excitement-seeking test, you will have a high drive for excitement-seeking. People who seek excitement like the idea of taking risk and chances. You enjoy finding opportunities and experiencing the feeling of exhilaration and accomplishment. You are an active person who strives to gain the most out of a situation. You love bright lights and this idea of 'hustle and bustle'. People who are excitement-seekers are people who get bored very quickly. You like to keep upbeat and face on-going challenges. Employers value people who take a little risk. However, you don't want to score an extreme score. Scoring an extreme score might suggest that you are reckless and irresponsible. You want to be able to show that you're the type of person who takes caution but also show a little risk in order to prevail.
AVERAGE (mostly 3's)	An average score means that you are on the borderline of seeking excitement. Although you are often considered careful and cautious, you do enjoy the occasional exciting thrill and/or risk. You do like routine and structure, but you are not stranger to taking the occasional chance every now and then. You like to face challenges and achieve your goals and ambitions in life. It is argued that you cannot get to where you want to be without taking a little risk every now and then, and you're the type of person who is able to do just that. You know when to take the risk and when to play it safe.

LOW (mostly 1's or 2's)	If you scored mostly 1's on the excitement-seeking test, you show extreme low levels as an excitement-seeker. You are a careful, cautious and considerate person, who often overthinks things before putting them into action. People who score a low score on the scale of this test, demonstrate personality traits of being overwhelmed, anxious and vigilant. You are the type of person who prefers the idea of comfort. You prefer to know where you stand. You like structure, stability and familiarity. You're not the type of person who will take risks that could jeopardise your position in the workforce. You want to aim for an average score. You want to be able to show that you can take risks in order to improve or enhance your position further. However, you don't want an extreme high score which might show lack in judgement and irresponsibility.

POSITIVE EMOTIONS

A clear way of distinguishing if a person is extroverted or introverted is to analyse their positive emotions. This shows their tendency and ability to experience positive emotions and cheerfulness which is a valuable attribute for any job profession.

People that show extreme high levels of positive emotions are considered as optimists. Optimistic people are positive, hopeful and cheerful. The scale measures the extent to which a person shows these feelings and positive moods which can be analysed by assessing a person's happiness, enthusiasm, joy and positivity.

Low scorers for positive emotions experience less positive emotions. Negative emotions are often linked to Neuroticism (discussed earlier in chapter 1). Low scorers tend to be seldom amused and find it difficult to show any positive emotions. They are not prone to such energetic and enthusiastic emotions and therefore are more reserved and more pessimistic.

These 30 questions will measure your level of positive emotions to help to determine your level of extroversion. The questions are simple; use the table below to answer the following questions. Circle the number that represents your answer and then use your answers to check your score.

Note: Reversed means that answering 'agree' or 'strongly agree' to the question will result in a low score of that trait.

1	2	3	4	5
Strongly Disagree	Disagree	Neutral	Agree	Strongly Agree

1. I often feel happy.

1	2	3	4	5

2. I seldom feel blue.

1	2	3	4	5

3. I consider myself a cheerful and contented person.

1	2	3	4	5

4. I am relaxed most of the time.

1	2	3	4	5

5. I have a positive attitude towards life.

1	2	3	4	5

6. I often wake up in a bad mood. (Reversed)

| 1 | 2 | 3 | 4 | 5 |

7. I am not easily upset.

| 1 | 2 | 3 | 4 | 5 |

8. I seldom get mad.

| 1 | 2 | 3 | 4 | 5 |

9. I have frequent mood swings. (Reversed)

| 1 | 2 | 3 | 4 | 5 |

10. I always have a good outlook on life.

| 1 | 2 | 3 | 4 | 5 |

11. I enjoy life.

| 1 | 2 | 3 | 4 | 5 |

12. People who are constantly in a bad mood annoy me.

| 1 | 2 | 3 | 4 | 5 |

13. I rarely get irritated.

| 1 | 2 | 3 | 4 | 5 |

14. I am hardly ever upset.

| 1 | 2 | 3 | 4 | 5 |

15. I have a short fuse. (Reversed)

| 1 | 2 | 3 | 4 | 5 |

16. I am happy and fulfilled with life.

| 1 | 2 | 3 | 4 | 5 |

17. People consider me to be naïve.

| 1 | 2 | 3 | 4 | 5 |

18. I generally anticipate for the best possible outcome.

| 1 | 2 | 3 | 4 | 5 |

19. I feel bright about my future.

1	2	3	4	5

20. I am always realistic, even if that means being negative. (Reversed)

1	2	3	4	5

21. I look for the best in people.

1	2	3	4	5

22. I often fear the worse. (Reversed)

1	2	3	4	5

23. Sometimes I think I am too positive for my own good.

1	2	3	4	5

24. Being pessimistic about everything will get you nowhere in life.

1	2	3	4	5

25. You have to have a good outlook on life.

1	2	3	4	5

26. My friends see me as the cheerful and optimist of the group.

1	2	3	4	5

27. Optimists are somewhat immature. (Reversed)

1	2	3	4	5

28. I experience positive emotions more than I do negative emotions.

1	2	3	4	5

29. I consider myself a positive person.

1	2	3	4	5

30. I believe everyone has something to be cheerful about.

1	2	3	4	5

Scoring System:

Circle the number that represents your chosen answer:

Note: make sure you circle the opposite answer from your above answer for the Reversed answers

1.	2.	3.	4.	5.
1 2 3 4 5	1 2 3 4 5	1 2 3 4 5	1 2 3 4 5	1 2 3 4 5
6. (R) 1 2 3 4 5	7. 1 2 3 4 5	8. 1 2 3 4 5	9. (R) 1 2 3 4 5	10. 1 2 3 4 5
11. 1 2 3 4 5	12. 1 2 3 4 5	13. 1 2 3 4 5	14. 1 2 3 4 5	15. (R) 1 2 3 4 5
16. 1 2 3 4 5	17. 1 2 3 4 5	18. 1 2 3 4 5	19. 1 2 3 4 5	20. (R) 1 2 3 4 5
21. 1 2 3 4 5	22. (R) 1 2 3 4 5	23. 1 2 3 4 5	24. 1 2 3 4 5	25. 1 2 3 4 5
26. 1 2 3 4 5	27. (R) 1 2 3 4 5	28. 1 2 3 4 5	29. 1 2 3 4 5	30. 1 2 3 4 5

SCORE TOTAL:	1's =	....	LOW
SCORE TOTAL:	2's =	....	
SCORE TOTAL:	3's =	....	AVERAGE
SCORE TOTAL:	4's =	....	
SCORE TOTAL:	5's =	....	HIGH

Circle your highest score.

Understanding Your Scores:

Your results on the positive emotions test will help determine your overall outcome for the trait of Extroversion. Once you've added up how many questions you answered strongly disagree, disagree, neutral, agree and strongly agree; it will be a clear way of distinguishing if your score was high, average or low.

If you answered mostly 5's or 4's, your score is going to demonstrate an extremely high level of trust. If you answered mostly 1's or 2's, your score is going to be extremely low. If you scored mostly 3's, you should read the average column.

HIGH (mostly 5's or 4's)	If you scored mostly 5's on the positive emotions test, this means you are a person who experiences positive emotions to a high level. Positive emotions are grounds for positive people. These emotions of happiness, enthusiasm, optimism are people who often radiate joy and have a positive attitude towards life. You are the type of person who rarely experiences negative emotions which is often linked to neurotic behaviour, and instead you use your positive emotions to express your thoughts and feelings. However, while employers often seek employers that show a good level of positive emotions and a positive attitude towards life and work; you do not want to score an extreme score on the scale. An extreme score in terms of positive emotions may suggest that you are somewhat naïve, immature and inexperienced. You need to maintain and be able to demonstrate your positive attitudes and emotions but also be able to show that you are in touch with reality and understand the boundaries between positivity and naivety.
AVERAGE (mostly 3's)	An average score for positive emotions means that you show both positivity and negativity in your responses from the above questions. A positive attitude will not only benefit the company, but also yourself. You will feel better as a person and begin to understand that a positive attitude towards life makes life more bearable and happier. However, you sometimes feel negative emotions and find it hard to be that optimistic person that you usually are. Most people experience negative feelings from time to time, and it is how you deal with these emotions that is important. These negative feelings are normal, but constant changes in mood might suggest to employers that you are unstable and not in the right frame of mind to work. You need to be able to show a healthy balance of positivity and negativity and deal with such emotions in a positive way.

LOW (mostly 1's or 2's)	If you scored mostly 1's on the positive emotions test, it suggests that you lack the ability to show a positive attitude. People who score a low score on the positive emotions test are the complete opposite to optimists. They demonstrate a pessimistic attitude towards life and find it difficult to show happy and enthusiastic emotions. You are the type of person who is not prone to breakouts of pure happiness and joy and therefore do not have such high spirits. You are seldom amused and thus come across as more candid and straight to the point. Having an extreme low score for positive emotions is an undesirable quality for most employers. Employers want to employ people who bring a positive vibe to the workforce and are able to demonstrate their positive feelings and emotions in order to provide a calm and comfortable environment. Depending on your job role and what is required of you, you still want to be able to show some levels of positivity. People who are pessimistic and overwhelmed by their emotions often make a work place feel uncomfortable and makes it a cause for concern amongst employers.

ACTIVITY

The final facet of assessing one's extroversion is this idea of activity. By activity we don't mean sporting or leisure activities, we simply refer to your lifestyle and your level of goings-on. Assessing a person's level of activity not only offers an insight into how busy their lifestyle is or whether they like to take it easy, it also indicates your work ethic and your ability to engage in the social world.

High scorers for their level of activity are extremely active people who are constantly on the go. They like to keep busy and lead fast-paced lifestyles. These people tend to move around quickly and energetically. They lead a vigorous way of life.

People who score a low score on the scales of activity often take a more laid back approach. They follow a slower and gentler pace rather than energetically going for it. They take their time and follow a more leisured and relaxed lifestyle.

These 30 questions will measure your level of activity to help to determine your level of extroversion. The questions are simple; use the table below to answer the following questions. Circle the number that represents your answer and then use your answers to check your score.

Note: Reversed means that answering 'agree' or 'strongly agree' to the question will result in a low score of that trait.

1	2	3	4	5
Strongly Disagree	Disagree	Neutral	Agree	Strongly Agree

1. I am always on the go.

1	2	3	4	5

2. I like to lead a busy lifestyle.

1	2	3	4	5

3. I am 'gone with the wind'.

1	2	3	4	5

4. Being busy is better than being bored.

1	2	3	4	5

5. Being busy is the fastest way to becoming successful.

1	2	3	4	5

6.   I don't often have free time.

| 1 | 2 | 3 | 4 | 5 |

7.   I often cancel plans because I have so much going on.

| 1 | 2 | 3 | 4 | 5 |

8.   Even when I finish work, I am still on the go.

| 1 | 2 | 3 | 4 | 5 |

9.   I lack motivation and energy. (Reversed)

| 1 | 2 | 3 | 4 | 5 |

10. I like to sit back and relax. (Reversed)

| 1 | 2 | 3 | 4 | 5 |

11. My lifestyle is hectic.

| 1 | 2 | 3 | 4 | 5 |

12. I need to create more free time.

| 1 | 2 | 3 | 4 | 5 |

13. I like to keep busy in order to get things done.

| 1 | 2 | 3 | 4 | 5 |

14. I am stressed because of how busy I am.

| 1 | 2 | 3 | 4 | 5 |

15. I continue working even when I get home.

| 1 | 2 | 3 | 4 | 5 |

16. I would do overtime in order to get closer to my goals.

| 1 | 2 | 3 | 4 | 5 |

17. I rarely have time to 'chill out'.

| 1 | 2 | 3 | 4 | 5 |

18. I take a slower approach to ensure accuracy. (Reversed)

| 1 | 2 | 3 | 4 | 5 |

19. I have plenty of free time. (Reversed)

1	2	3	4	5

20. I maintain a vigorous lifestyle.

1	2	3	4	5

21. I like to keep busy in order to take my mind off things.

1	2	3	4	5

22. I do the very least possible. (Reversed)

1	2	3	4	5

23. I am often calm and do not feel as though I am rushed. (Reversed)

1	2	3	4	5

24. A busy lifestyle at home suggests I will lead a busy lifestyle at work.

1	2	3	4	5

25. I often feel full of energy.

1	2	3	4	5

26. I don't like that I am busy, but I am.

1	2	3	4	5

27. I often find myself tired and stressed out.

1	2	3	4	5

28. I feel dynamic in everything I do.

1	2	3	4	5

29. I am unable to work at a faster pace. (Reversed)

1	2	3	4	5

30. I consider myself a person who is full of life, full of energy and constantly on the go.

1	2	3	4	5

Scoring System:

Circle the number that represents your chosen answer:

Note: make sure you circle the opposite answer from your above answer for the Reversed answers

1.	2.	3.	4.	5.
1 2 3 4 5	1 2 3 4 5	1 2 3 4 5	1 2 3 4 5	1 2 3 4 5
6.	7.	8.	9.	10.
1 2 3 4 5	1 2 3 4 5	1 2 3 4 5	(R) 1 2 3 4 5	(R) 1 2 3 4 5
11.	12.	13.	14.	15.
1 2 3 4 5	1 2 3 4 5	1 2 3 4 5	1 2 3 4 5	1 2 3 4 5
16.	17.	18.	19.	20.
1 2 3 4 5	1 2 3 4 5	(R) 1 2 3 4 5	(R) 1 2 3 4 5	1 2 3 4 5
21.	22.	23.	24.	25.
1 2 3 4 5	(R) 1 2 3 4 5	(R) 1 2 3 4 5	1 2 3 4 5	1 2 3 4 5
26.	27.	28.	29.	30.
1 2 3 4 5	1 2 3 4 5	1 2 3 4 5	(R) 1 2 3 4 5	1 2 3 4 5

SCORE TOTAL:	1's =	....	LOW
SCORE TOTAL:	2's =	....	
SCORE TOTAL:	3's =	....	AVERAGE
SCORE TOTAL:	4's =	....	
SCORE TOTAL:	5's =	....	HIGH

Circle your highest score.

Understanding Your Scores:

Your results on the level of activity test will help determine your overall outcome for the trait of Extroversion. Once you've added up how many questions you answered strongly disagree, disagree, neutral, agree and strongly agree; it will be a clear way of distinguishing if your score was high, average or low.

If you answered mostly 5's or 4's, your score is going to demonstrate an extremely high level of trust. If you answered mostly 1's or 2's, your score is going to be extremely low. If you scored mostly 3's, you should read the average column.

HIGH (mostly 5's or 4's)	If you scored mostly 5's on your level of activity test, this indicates that you have an extremely active and busy lifestyle. You like to keep busy. You like to always be on the go and get things done as quickly and efficiently as possible. Your vigorous lifestyle means you have little time to stop and think and just relax. You have little free time, and more often than not, you enjoy maintaining this way of life. Your fast-paced lifestyle reinforces your ability to demonstrate energy and enthusiasm. Maintaining an active and busy lifestyle reassures employers that you get the job done and you don't take it lightly. By demonstrating that you work at a fast-pace is desirable for employers. They like to maintain an efficient and stable work environment. However, you do not want to work at such a fast-pace that you lose your ability to do it to the best standard. You want to make sure that you work quickly whilst still maintaining accuracy and not jeopardising the outcome.
AVERAGE (mostly 3's)	An average score for level of activity means that your work life and home life are pretty much balanced. Some days maybe extremely busy and this means that you're always on the go, whereas other days might be much slower and calmer and more relaxed. You are able to balance your time efficiently and do not feel overwhelmed by the daily tasks and jobs you have to do. You get on with your work efficiently and do not often feel rushed, although this may change according to how hectic your day at work is. You are often considered laid back, but you show capabilities of moving at a faster pace when the situation requires you to do so.

LOW **(mostly** **1's or 2's)**	If you scored mostly 1's on your level of activity, it suggests that you lead a very calm and relaxed lifestyle.

Unlike leading a fast-paced and active lifestyle, you tend to take your time and take a slower approach.

Your slower approach might indicate to employers that your work ethic is not up to scratch. Employers like to be assured that when required, you are able to get something done and do it by the deadline they give you. You don't want to go over the deadline and not be finished because this shows lack of enthusiasm and unprofessionalism.

Although working at a slower pace might indicate that you are thorough and more accurate, it might also show a sign of laziness and the inability to work to deadlines.

Therefore, you need to be able to show some level of activity that demonstrates your work ethic and the ability to work to deadlines and in stressful situations. However, you also want to maintain accuracy, validity and precision. |

How Extroverted Are You?

So, you've finished answering all the questions on Extroversion. We have provided the table below to generate a general understanding of your level of extroverted.

Now go back through the six sub-traits for Extroversion and use your high, average and low scores to fill in the table below.

TRAIT	Warmth	Gregari-ous-ness	Asser-tive-ness	Excitement Seeking	Positive Emotions	Level of Activity
HIGH, AVERAGE OR LOW?						

What does this mean overall?

HIGH	Extroversion shows high levels of sociability. You are a social person who enjoys the company of other people. You show traits of friendliness and warmth and have a genuine interest in getting to know other people.

You are the type of person who is often referred to in psychology as an extrovert. You are a dynamic, outgoing and active person who seeks companionship and social interaction. Extroverts don't often like being on their own, and feel the need to be around people.

Depending on your job role and the type of personality traits that are desirable, employers are more than likely looking for people who show traits of extroversion.

Traits such as motivation, enthusiasm and optimism will benefit most companies. They like to be assured of valuable team members.

TRAITS = energetic, enthusiastic, assertive, motivated, talkative, friendly, optimistic |

AVERAGE	Scoring an average score suggests that you are both extroverted and introverted. You are able to show levels of both traits and therefore suggest your flexibility and adaptability to change when the situation requires.

Although you are somewhat reserved when it comes to the people around you, you are able to make yourself approachable and friendly when necessary.

Even though you may show characteristics of shyness and reserved, you also come across as sociable and outgoing.

You do not mind whether you have companionship or if you are by yourself, you are able to adapt to either situation and get on with the situation accordingly.

Employers like to see people not only show the ability to show friendliness, compassion and social interaction, but also people who are able to work on their own initiative and do not have to rely on other people.

TRAITS = friendliness, optimistic, independent, confident, compliant, reserved |
| **LOW** | People who score a low score overall on extroversion suggests that they are more introverted as opposed to extroverted. You are very reserved. You like to remain independent and you enjoy being on your own.

You find it difficult to interact with people and struggle to 'fit in' and comprehend the idea of mixing with other people.

Introverts are often described as shy, reserved and aloof. You tend to withdraw from large crowds and take preference of being distant and independent.

People who score low in regards to extroversion are better suited to jobs that don't require much social interaction. You find it difficult to interact with others and so a career that requires that, would not suit you and you would not suit the job.

TRAITS = aloof, shy, reserved, pessimistic, introverted, distant |

What does this say to employers about your personality?

A person who is willing to interact and enjoy social experiences is a person that most employers value. They like to see people who are team players. They like to see their employees apply a friendly and gregarious approach which helps maintain a comfortable working environment.

You want to be able to show that you can apply yourself in a situation that requires you to engage with different social relations. You want to show employers that you take pride in your ability to succeed. An extroverted person needs to maintain a balance of such traits as enthusiasm and assertiveness, but not come across as arrogant and over-confident. Find the right balance between extroversion and introversion and aim for an average score. Try not to score extremely high or extremely low – it will only show that you're the type of person who finds change difficult.

CHAPTER 4 - The Big 5:

Conscientiousness

CHAPTER 4 - THE BIG 5: CONSCIENTIOUSNESS

If there is one personality trait that you want to shine through is this idea of conscientiousness. It is the personality trait that demonstrates a person's ability to show vigilance, thoroughness and careful deliberations; an attribute that most employers desire. Conscientious people are able to follow instruction, complete their tasks, meet deadlines and illustrate high levels of commitment and work ethic.

Employers seek people who have a high level of conscientiousness. People who are conscientious avoid trouble and demonstrate great levels of self-control and efficiency. They are people who are often thought of as reliable, independent and cautious. They are concerned with purposefulness and persistence.

People who score a low score for conscientiousness are criticised for their lack of thinking. Sometimes they don't think about their actions or the consequences of their behaviour. They are often considered as unreliable and lack ambition and structure.

Conscientiousness also refers to people's impulses. The way in which we control and regulate and direct our impulses is important. Impulses are not always bad; there may be a time where a situation requires you to act on a quick impulse and make a rash decision. However, acting on an impulse can sometimes lead to trouble. It may produce results which take an immediate effect but have long term repercussions. Therefore, finding the right balance between an adequate conscientiousness that allows for quickness and efficiency, but also remains rational and thorough is crucial.

There are several sub-traits that personality tests look at to measure conscientiousness. These indicate behaviour traits that form part of a person's personality, which are often analysed in terms of **competence, order, dutifulness, self-discipline, deliberation and achievement-striving.**

In this chapter, it will focus on each one of these terms and assess your personality to determine your level of conscientiousness.

COMPETENCE

When personality tests refer to the term conscientiousness, it often tests a person's level of competence. Competence can be used to describe a person's capabilities. In other words, it demonstrates what level that person is self-efficient and how well they manage to accomplish set work and other tasks.

People with high levels of competence believe they have great intellectual skills. They also believe that they have the drive, ambition and self-control necessary for successfully reaching their goals.

Low scorers often misjudge situations and find it difficult to complete tasks to a high standard. Low scores sometimes demonstrate the inability to take control. They are depicted as people who do not have control of their lives, and therefore are uncertain about what to do. People with low competence feel ineffective. They believe they make no contribution or effort to the job at hand and therefore lack motivation and self-esteem.

These 30 questions will measure your level of competence and help to determine your level of conscientiousness. The questions are simple; circle true or false to the statements provided and then use your answers to check your score.

Note: Reversed means that answering 'true' to the question will result in a low score of that trait.

1. I consider myself an intellectual person.

    | True | False |

2. I rarely misjudge a situation.

    | True | False |

3. I tend to take my time on set tasks. (Reversed)

    | True | False |

4. I have confidence with the tasks that I am set.

    | True | False |

5. I always feel confident.

    | True | False |

6. I complete my work to the highest standard.

| True | False |

7. I would describe myself as extremely self-efficient.

| True | False |

8. I like to get things done as quickly as possible.

| True | False |

9. I often struggle with completing my work to a high standard. (Reversed)

| True | False |

10. Seldom, I have to ask for help with my work.

| True | False |

11. I am adaptable.

| True | False |

12. I don't rely on other people.

| True | False |

13. I have the necessary ability and knowledge to do my work successfully.

| True | False |

14. All my work is proficient.

| True | False |

15. I am a sufficient worker.

| True | False |

16. I always look deeper into my work to gain more knowledge.

| True | False |

17. I do not put 100% into everything I do. (Reversed)

| True | False |

18. I am able to assist others and offer my expertise and knowledge.

| True | False |

19. I do not feel like I am properly qualified. (Reversed)

True	False

20. I try to exceed expectations

True	False

21. I can handle a lot of information.

True	False

22. I find it difficult to get down to work. (Reversed)

True	False

23. I will not probe deeply into my work. (Reversed)

True	False

24. I read difficult reading material to help with my job.

True	False

25. I am able to work without any help.

True	False

26. Working hard is rewarding.

True	False

27. I do not require further training.

True	False

28. I have control of my life and my workload.

True	False

29. I like completing tasks and accomplishing something.

True	False

30. I consider myself a capable person.

True	False

Scoring System:

Circle the letter that represents your chosen answer:

Note: make sure you circle the opposite answer from your above answer for the Reversed answers

1. T / F	**2.** T / F	**3.** T / F *(R)*	**4.** T / F	**5.** T / F
6. T / F	**7.** T / F	**8.** T / F	**9.** T / F *(R)*	**10.** T / F
11. T / F	**12.** T / F	**13.** T / F	**14.** T / F	**15.** T / F
16. T / F	**17.** T / F *(R)*	**18.** T / F	**19.** T / F *(R)*	**20.** T / F
21. T / F	**22.** T / F *(R)*	**23.** T / F *(R)*	**24.** T / F	**25.** T / F
26. T / F	**27.** T / F	**28.** T / F	**29.** T / F	**30.** T / F

SCORE TOTAL:	True =	....	HIGH
SCORE TOTAL:	False =	....	LOW

Understanding Your Scores:

Your results on the Competence test will help determine your overall outcome for the trait of Conscientiousness. Once you've added up how many questions you answered true to, and how many questions you answered false, it will be a clear way of distinguishing if your score was high, average or low.

If you answered true to most of the questions, then below is a detailed explanation of what this means. If you answered false to most questions, then read the description for what a low response means. An average score considers both low and high traits, so therefore you should read that description.

HIGH (mostly true)	If you answered mostly true to the questions, it shows high levels of competence. You are a capable, knowledgeable and independent person who is able to complete work to the highest standard. You are confident and capable of offering your knowledge and expertise in a subject matter and you feel like you are somewhat qualified to mentor other people who need a little more help. People who show high levels of competency show great determination and ambition; traits that employers value to see. You do not want to gain an extreme score in competence as this might suggest arrogance and egotism. People can always improve. They can always get better. So, being a competent person doesn't mean you can stop trying. You want to show that whilst you have great knowledge and understanding, you want to be able to demonstrate that you are willing to excel in your performance, without arrogance being an issue.
AVERAGE	An average score for competence illustrates that you show a balanced level of competency. You show that you are capable and knowledgeable and are able to work independently. You may question your work or believe your work is not to a high enough standard, but this reinforces your critical thinking and ability to evaluate your own work, however critical or harsh you are on yourself. Competency comes with time. You are able to work on your skills and knowledge to provide the expertise you have gained so far.

LOW (mostly false)	Mostly false answers indicate that you lack competence. People who lack competence tend to suffer with confidence issues and lack of self-belief. This might be because you feel like you are not good enough or simply that you are not ready. You find it difficult to work to a high standard and feel as though your work is 'ineffective'. You don't have the confidence or self-efficiency to believe in your own work without criticising it. Competence can be worked on. You can improve your abilities and demonstrate a higher success rate. You need to gain the knowledge, experience and the confidence to know that you are not only good at what you do, but great! Employers like to see some levels of competence and so you need to aim for an average score. Employers like to be assured that their workforce is full of competent people who can bring their best work forward to enhance the business and reach success.

ORDER

Conscientiousness also refers to the ability of being logical and organised. Order is a key facet that allows key traits to be assessed in terms of organisation, planning and routine. By demonstrating order, it indicates your level of precision and structure.

People who score highly on order are people who are extremely well-organised. High scorers are neat and tidy. They like the idea of structure, scheduling and routine. They keep lists and make plans and run a smooth and effective working system.

Low scorers tend not to worry about organisation. Low scorers are people who are disorganised and lead a 'scattered' lifestyle. They do not worry about where they have placed things, or writing things down to remember; they often leave a mess and get on with things.

These 30 questions will measure your level of orderliness and help to determine your level of conscientiousness. The questions are simple; circle true or false to the statements provided and then use your answers to check your score.

Note: Reversed means that answering 'true' to the question will result in a low score of that trait.

1. I rarely lose important documents.

   | True | False |

2. I am always prepared.

   | True | False |

3. I stick to my plans like glue.

   | True | False |

4. I like routine.

   | True | False |

5. I make plans and mind-maps.

   | True | False |

6. I am an organised person.

   | True | False |

7. I dislike it if someone moves something out of place.

True	False

8. I follow a schedule.

True	False

9. I often find myself losing things. (Reversed)

True	False

10. I make a mess of things. (Reversed)

True	False

11. I often put things back in their correct place.

True	False

12. Routine is boring. (Reversed)

True	False

13. I like structure.

True	False

14. I never stray from my plans.

True	False

15. I keep everything in its place and know where everything is.

True	False

16. I never plan ahead. (Reversed)

True	False

17. Routine makes me feel secure and confident.

True	False

18. I rarely lose my keys or mobile.

True	False

19. If my boss wanted to see an important document, I would know exactly where it is.

True	False

20. I am neat and tidy.

True	False

21. I am slightly obsessive with tidiness and organisation.

True	False

22. I find it difficult to stray from my normal routine.

True	False

23. Preparation is the key to success.

True	False

24. I don't often think about where I have placed something. (Reversed)

True	False

25. I get annoyed if a picture frame is askew.

True	False

26. I have to move something if it is slightly out of place.

True	False

27. I write things down to remember them.

True	False

28. I am thorough in everything I do.

True	False

29. I like to know what I am doing every day.

True	False

30. I run a smooth and organised lifestyle.

True	False

Scoring System:

Circle the letter that represents your chosen answer:

Note: make sure you circle the opposite answer from your above answer for the Reversed answers

1.	T / F	**2.**	T / F	**3.**	T / F	**4.**	T / F	**5.**	T / F
6.	T / F	**7.**	T / F	**8.**	T / F	**9.** *(R)*	T / F	**10.** *(R)*	T / F
11.	T / F	**12.** *(R)*	T / F	**13.**	T / F	**14.**	T / F	**15.**	T / F
16. *(R)*	T / F	**17.**	T / F	**18.**	T / F	**19.**	T / F	**20.**	T / F
21.	T / F	**22.**	T / F	**23.**	T / F	**24.** *(R)*	T / F	**25.**	T / F
26.	T / F	**27.**	T / F	**28.**	T / F	**29.**	T / F	**30.**	T / F

SCORE TOTAL:	True =	....	HIGH
SCORE TOTAL:	False =	....	LOW

Understanding Your Scores:

Your results on the Orderliness test will help determine your overall outcome for the trait of Conscientiousness. Once you've added up how many questions you answered true to, and how many questions you answered false, it will be a clear way of distinguishing if your score was high, average or low.

If you answered true to most of the questions, then below is a detailed explanation of what this means. If you answered false to most questions, then read the description for what a low response means. An average score considers both low and high traits, so therefore you should read that description.

HIGH (mostly true)	If you scored mostly true on this test, this means that you have high levels of orderliness. The trait of order and organisation is important amongst most roles. It demonstrates your capabilities of following a routine and structure that ensures that you know what you are doing. Following routines, plans and lists makes you feel confident. It makes you feel secure and in control. Good organisation is one of many skills that employers often refer to. It allows them to understand how well you can work in a structured environment and how well you are able to organise your day in order to finish the work required. However, scoring extremely high on this can be a disadvantage. An extreme high score might suggest that you are incapable of change which might indicate a compulsive personality disorder. A high score indicates the tendency of becoming too stressed if your plan doesn't go as planned, and therefore you feel the sense of failure and disappointment.
AVERAGE	An average score for order means that you show both high and low levels of being able to follow order and structure. Generally, you find it easy to listen and follow instruction. You believe routine provides a secure and controlled way of doing things. You are an organised person, you plan your days, you know what has to be done and you present yourself as being in control. However, sometimes you find yourself as more carefree. You don't worry about putting things back in the right order or making plans, you just go ahead and get on with it. Sometimes a situation requires you to think fast and therefore there is no time to make plans. You are the type of person who is capable of adapting your usual everyday routine and produce active results instead.

LOW (mostly false)	If you scored mostly false for this test, this indicates that you find it difficult to follow order and structure. You are the type of person who does not worry about putting things back in the right place, or listing down things you need to do, or neatly place important documents on your desk. You take a more relaxed approach and therefore show a carefree spirit. You are often messy. You show traits of being a disorganised person and therefore often lose things or can't remember something you were meant to do. An extreme low score on the dimension of this scale is not recommended and not desirable for most employers. Employers like to employ a workforce that ensures an effective and smooth-running working environment. A low score might suggest that you are absent-minded; that you don't like to plan ahead and you often misplace things. Depending on your job role and the personality traits required, you still want to be able to show that you can follow instruction, that you can make plans and work efficiently as possible.

DUTIFULNESS

Within the working environment, a person needs to be able to express their sense of duty. The term **dutifulness** is a facet of conscientiousness that enables employers and businesses to understand how well a person can follow rules, in order to fulfil their obligations as an employee. You have an obligation to listen to instruction and to follow orders.

People with high levels of dutifulness often feel a great sense of obligation towards others. They like to follow the rules and complete their tasks. They have a strong idea of morals that adhere to their ethical principles and values. They often comply with the rules that are set and follow instruction without rebellion.

Low scorers are people who like to break the rules and often 'do their own thing'. They find contracts, rules and regulations extremely limiting and confining. They are likely to be described as immature, irresponsible and unreliable. They struggle to follow instruction and dislike the idea of being controlled by the rules of authority.

These 30 questions will measure your level of dutifulness and help to determine your level of conscientiousness. The questions are simple; circle true or false to the statements provided and then use your answers to check your score.

Note: Reversed means that answering 'true' to the question will result in a low score of that trait.

1. I follow instructions well.

True	False

2. I feel a strong sense of moral obligation at work.

True	False

3. I was often disciplined at school. (Reversed)

True	False

4. I do not like to get into trouble at work.

True	False

5. I keep myself to myself to ensure no trouble.

True	False

6. I come across as irresponsible and unreliable. (Reversed)

| True | False |

7. I find rules limiting. (Reversed)

| True | False |

8. I comply with the rules and regulations at work.

| True | False |

9. Rules are not there to be broken.

| True | False |

10. The people in my household know the rules.

| True | False |

11. We have an obligation to our employers.

| True | False |

12. The freedom to do what I want is very important to me. (Reversed)

| True | False |

13. I like following a set structure and routine.

| True | False |

14. I often break the rules. (Reversed)

| True | False |

15. I follow the rules even if I don't agree with them.

| True | False |

16. People consider me as reliable and mature.

| True | False |

17. We all have obligations to the people we work with.

| True | False |

18. I would rather follow instruction than do things my own way.

| True | False |

19. I consider myself an obedient person.

True	False

20. I feel comfortable following instruction.

True	False

21. I like to get things done.

True	False

22. I refuse to follow the rules if I don't agree with them. (Reversed)

True	False

23. I often rebel against things I don't agree with. (Reversed)

True	False

24. If someone asks me to do something, I usually do it.

True	False

25. I have a duty to myself and to my colleagues.

True	False

26. Rules are there for a reason.

True	False

27. I believe I am a compliant worker.

True	False

28. I don't like people telling me what to do. (Reversed)

True	False

29. I seldom disagree with what I am told.

True	False

30. I do my work without questioning it.

True	False

Scoring System:

Circle the letter that represents your chosen answer:

Note: make sure you circle the opposite answer from your above answer for the Reversed answers

1. T / F	2. T / F	3. T / F (R)	4. T / F	5. T / F
6. T / F (R)	7. T / F (R)	8. T / F	9. T / F	10. T / F
11. T / F	12. T / F (R)	13. T / F	14. T / F (R)	15. T / F
16. T / F	17. T / F	18. T / F	19. T / F	20. T / F
21. T / F	22. T / F (R)	23. T / F (R)	24. T / F	25. T / F
26. T / F	27. T / F	28. T / F (R)	29. T / F	30. T / F

SCORE TOTAL:	True = ...	HIGH
SCORE TOTAL:	False = ...	LOW

Understanding Your Scores:

Your results on the dutifulness test will help determine your overall outcome for the trait of Conscientiousness. Once you've added up how many questions you answered true to, and how many questions you answered false, it will be a clear way of distinguishing if your score was high, average or low.

If you answered true to most of the questions, then below is a detailed explanation of what this means. If you answered false to most questions, then read the description for what a low response means. An average score considers both low and high traits, so therefore you should read that description.

HIGH (mostly true)	If you scored mostly true on the dutifulness test, it means that you have high levels of dutifulness. You have a sense the moral obligations and underlying principles that are expected of you as an employee. You have a strong sense of duty to yourself, your co-workers and your employers. You follow the rules and don't deviate from them. You are a person who is obedient and reliable. You are given instructions and you follow them. You don't argue, you just get it done. Employers seek high scores for dutifulness to ensure maximum business potential. Employees who show that they are capable of following instruction and keep to the rules are desirable and admirable qualities. These qualities allow you as a worker to demonstrate high levels of perseverance and willingness to do what you are told.
AVERAGE	An average score for dutifulness means that you answered your questions in a balanced way. You show that you have a duty to the people around you. You show that you have a duty to the company you work for. Therefore, you feel a sense of moral obligation and respect. However, occasionally you find yourself acting on impulsive thoughts. You sometimes find yourself breaking the rules in order to prove a point or get your voice heard. Overall, you demonstrate a great level of dutifulness and indicate that whilst you are happy to follow instruction and the rules provided, you are not afraid to go against them if the situation requires.

LOW (mostly false)	People who score a low score on the dutifulness test are considered undesirable. People who show lack of obedience and duty towards their fellow workers and employers show traits of laziness and impulsiveness. You find rules and regulations extremely limiting. You do not like being confined through structure and hierarchy. You are unable to follow instruction and dislike being told what to do. You feel no sense of moral obligation or duty towards anyone else but yourself. Therefore you lack the skills to work in an environment that is team based. Employers find disobedient people unattractive, undesirable and unruly. They believe these people to be arrogant and superior to others. Thus, you want to score an average score that allows employers to see that you can be dutiful and you can obey instructions.

SELF-DISCIPLINE

Self-discipline is an excellent way to determine a person's motivational skills and persistence. The term self-discipline is often referred to as 'will power'. People who show the 'will power' to persist at difficult or boring tasks without giving up show great levels of self-discipline. Self-discipline is being able to start a task and see it all the way through, despite any complications or level of difficulty.

People who possess high levels of self-discipline and 'will power' are people who persevere. They are highly driven; they are motivated; they engage with tasks despite their lack of interest. They are able to get the work done with little distraction and not let boredom stop them from completing the task. It shows high resilience and work ethic that employers value a great deal.

Low scorers of self-discipline lack the motivation and energy to finish a task. These people show poor follow-through and demonstrate their incapability of seeing a project from beginning to completion. They let things easily distract them and often procrastinate their time.

These 30 questions will measure your level of self-discipline and help to determine your level of conscientiousness. The questions are simple; circle true or false to the statements provided and then use your answers to check your score.

Note: Reversed means that answering 'true' to the question will result in a low score of that trait.

1. I get chores done right away.

True	False

2. I work effectively and efficiently as possible.

True	False

3. I like to get my work done on time.

True	False

4. I like to finish the tasks that I am set.

True	False

5. I have high levels of 'will power'.

True	False

6. I find it difficult to motivate myself. (Reversed)

True	False

7. I am not easily distracted.

True	False

8. I complete my tasks to the best of my ability.

True	False

9. I often hand my work in before the deadline.

True	False

10. I will do the tasks I am set, even if I don't enjoy it.

True	False

11. I like to see projects through from beginning to end.

True	False

12. If I have no interest in something, I won't do it. (Reversed)

True	False

13. I often find myself procrastinating. (Reversed)

True	False

14. I set ambitions for myself and stick to them.

True	False

15. If I am given a job, I will do it.

True	False

16. I motivate myself to get the job done.

True	False

17. I am always an efficient worker.

True	False

18. I give 100% in everything I do.

True	False

19. I don't like wasting my time doing something I don't like. (Reversed)

| True | False |

20. I don't let boredom and distraction get in the way with what I have to do.

| True | False |

21. I don't like delaying my work.

| True | False |

22. I am an extremely driven person.

| True | False |

23. I hardly ever get distracted.

| True | False |

24. I believe I am a self-disciplined person.

| True | False |

25. I make myself a strict schedule and stick to it in order to get my work done.

| True | False |

26. I always get my work done on time.

| True | False |

27. I often have to ask for an extension to complete my tasks. (Reversed)

| True | False |

28. I persevere in everything I do.

| True | False |

29. Despite lack of interest, I will still take on the task.

| True | False |

30. I consider myself a persistent, reliable and motivated person.

| True | False |

Scoring System:

Circle the letter that represents your chosen answer:

Note: make sure you circle the opposite answer from your above answer for the Reversed answers

1. T / F	**2.** T / F	**3.** T / F	**4.** T / F	**5.** T / F
6. T / F *(R)*	**7.** T / F	**8.** T / F	**9.** T / F	**10.** T / F
11. T / F	**12.** T / F *(R)*	**13.** T / F *(R)*	**14.** T / F	**15.** T / F
16. T / F	**17.** T / F	**18.** T / F	**19.** T / F *(R)*	**20.** T / F
21. T / F	**22.** T / F	**23.** T / F	**24.** T / F	**25.** T / F
26. T / F	**27.** T / F *(R)*	**28.** T / F	**29.** T / F	**30.** T / F

SCORE TOTAL:	True =	....	HIGH
SCORE TOTAL:	False =	....	LOW

Understanding Your Scores:

Your results on the self-discipline test will help determine your overall outcome for the trait of Conscientiousness. Once you've added up how many questions you answered true to, and how many questions you answered false, it will be a clear way of distinguishing if your score was high, average or low.

If you answered true to most of the questions, then below is a detailed explanation of what this means. If you answered false to most questions, then read the description for what a low response means. An average score considers both low and high traits, so therefore you should read that description.

HIGH (mostly true)	If you scored mostly true for this test, you are considered a highly self-disciplined person. You are capable of demonstrating sheer 'will power' and determination. You are motivated, highly driven and capable of completing tasks. Even if you have a lack of interest in the subject area or you struggle with it; you persevere. You are persistent and carry on and overcome any obstacles. Highly self-disciplined people show the ability to work effectively and logically. You need little guidance from others and they don't need to be given motivation by others. Employers value people who show great self-disciplinary skills. It enables them to gain insight into how people will respond when they are given a challenge. They will be able to see who will go that extra mile to complete the job, despite how undesirable it may be.
AVERAGE	An average score for self-discipline shows that you are not only motivated, driven and capable, but also demonstrate some levels of reluctance and procrastination. Whilst most people would not admit that they procrastinate their time at work and leave things to the last minute, this test suggests that you sometimes do this. However, you are driven and motivated to complete the tasks done, and even if you leave it to later, you never fail to get the work done. You're often a logical and effective worker who takes little guidance from others. However, you are not afraid to ask for help when you do need it.

LOW (mostly false)	If you scored mostly false for the test on self-discipline, it shows that you lack any 'will power'. You find it difficult to take on tasks that you don't want or that you don't have any interest in. You show little motivation and perseverance in getting the job done. Low scorers tend to be people who procrastinate. They usually leave the job until the last minute or put it off altogether. Employers view people with low self-discipline as extremely reluctant. They see them as unwilling and somewhat arrogant. Employers like to know that they are employing people who will take on a challenge. They like people who are 'triers'. Even if they don't succeed, employers value someone who tried and failed more than someone who was reluctant at doing it in the first place. You need to show some level of self-discipline in order to display self-control, incentive and willingness.

DELIBERATION

Another significant facet for assessing one's conscientiousness is deliberation. Deliberation is a term used to test how much a person thinks before they speak or act out. In simpler terms, people who show that they are deliberated are people who show great levels of cautiousness. Cautiousness describes the disposition of avoiding mistakes and not rushing into things. They take their time to consider the possibilities.

People who possess high levels of deliberation are extremely cautious people. They often think and mull things over before they say them out loud or put them into action. They have the tendency to overthink – to analyse and interpret rather than act on initial thoughts and impulses.

Low scorers of deliberation are the complete opposite. They don't think things through and therefore act on quick thought. People with low deliberation are spontaneous. They often make hasty and quick decisions. They say and do the first things that come into mind, without deliberating alternative ideas and not foreseeing that their actions have consequences.

These 30 questions will measure your level of deliberation and help to determine your level of conscientiousness. The questions are simple; circle true or false to the statements provided and then use your answers to check your score.

Note: Reversed means that answering 'true' to the question will result in a low score of that trait.

1. I take the time to critically analyse something.

| True | False |

2. I often mull things over.

| True | False |

3. People consider me a wary person.

| True | False |

4. I like to avoid making mistakes.

| True | False |

5. I tend not to rush into things.

| True | False |

6. I often worry about my actions.

True	False

7. I hardly ever make mistakes.

True	False

8. I am not a careless person.

True	False

9. People would often describe me as spontaneous. (Reversed)

True	False

10. I usually notice when an idea isn't good.

True	False

11. I often make mistakes. (Reversed)

True	False

12. I think before I act.

True	False

13. I have the tendency to over think things.

True	False

14. When I have made a decision, I often worry if I made the right one.

True	False

15. I work very thoroughly and logically.

True	False

16. I consider things from all angles.

True	False

17. I often rush into things. (Reversed)

True	False

18. I always worry about my work.

True	False

19. I constantly write and re-write most of my work.

True	False

20. I would consider myself a cautious person.

True	False

21. I am alert and aware of my actions.

True	False

22. I am not a spontaneous person.

True	False

23. I don't like risks.

True	False

24. I take the time to research something before I take it any further.

True	False

25. I am quite hesitant with my job.

True	False

26. I don't make rash decisions.

True	False

27. I worry about the consequences of my actions.

True	False

28. I am an unhurried and thorough person.

True	False

29. I am an extremely logical and rational person.

True	False

30. I find it difficult to not overthink things.

True	False

Scoring System:

Circle the letter that represents your chosen answer:

Note: make sure you circle the opposite answer from your above answer for the Reversed answers

1.	T / F	2.	T / F	3.	T / F	4.	T / F	5.	T / F
6.	T / F	7.	T / F	8.	T / F	9. (R)	T / F	10.	T / F
11. (R)	T / F	12.	T / F	13.	T / F	14.	T / F	15.	T / F
16.	T / F	17. (R)	T / F	18.	T / F	19.	T / F	20.	T / F
21.	T / F	22.	T / F	23.	T / F	24.	T / F	25.	T / F
26.	T / F	27.	T / F	28.	T / F	29.	T / F	30.	T / F

SCORE TOTAL:	True =	....	HIGH
SCORE TOTAL:	False =	....	LOW

Understanding Your Scores:

Change first and second paragraphs with these: Your results on the deliberation test will help determine your overall outcome for the trait of Conscientiousness. Once you've added up how many questions you answered true to, and how many questions you answered false, it will be a clear way of distinguishing if your score was high, average or low.

If you answered true to most of the questions, then below is a detailed explanation of what this means. If you answered false to most questions, then read the description for what a low response means. An average score considers both low and high traits, so therefore you should read that description.

HIGH (mostly true)	If you scored mostly true, you are a highly deliberate person. You are cautious. You take caution in everything you do. You like to do your job and you like to do it well. You mull things over and don't rush into anything too quickly. You take your time to ensure the best standard of work and the best possible outcome. You analyse and overthink things which is often seen as a good thing. You are able to interpret and look deeper into things without making a hasty decision. You are thorough and efficient. You demonstrate high levels of critical thinking and the ability to illustrate your work ethic. However, you do not want to score an extreme score. Scoring an extreme high score might suggest to employers that you are unable to quickly think on your feet and offer quick responses.
AVERAGE	An average score on deliberation means that you sometimes show your cautiousness, but also show your impulsiveness. You are considered a cautious person. Although you might not take caution in everything you do, you like to ensure that you have thoroughly looked at something before going ahead and doing it. However, sometimes a situation requires you to act quickly, and therefore you are able to act on your initial impulse. You can show employers that you are capable of thinking fast and acting quickly when necessary. You need to show a balance between a great working ability that demonstrates your critical thinking, cautiousness and the ability to analyse something without rushing into it, but also are able to show that you can offer quick responses when required.

LOW (mostly false)	If you scored mostly false, you have low deliberation and cautiousness.

Unlike people who are deliberated, you tend not to worry about things. You don't feel the need to mull things over and take caution in everything you do.

You act on impulse. You usually take your initial idea and get stuck in with it. You do not take the time to think about alternative possibilities. You don't take the time to think about that your actions have consequences, despite the best intentions.

People who score a low score for deliberation are people often described as spontaneous. You are the type of person who is impulsive and act on the 'spur-of-the-moment'.

Employers want to see that you are capable of thinking about your actions. They want to be assured of people who won't jeopardise a situation by acting on initial impulses.

You need to be able to show that whilst you can act on quick thinking and take a carefree approach, you also want to show that you are thorough and cautious. Not every idea is a great idea. Therefore, you need to know what ideas are great ideas and what ideas are a waste of time. |

ACHIEVEMENT-STRIVING

Conscientiousness also looks at people's achievement striving levels to assess their level of ambition and determination. Individuals who have aspirations and goals seek to achieve and accomplish their targets and objectives. Individuals who possess the trait of achievement striving have the tendency to strive greatly to achieve excellence.

People with high levels of striving for achievement are the people who want to work hard and achieve something. They have the 'will power' and the drive to excel in their performance in order to be recognised as successful and worthy. This allows them to keep motivated and on track with their life ambitions. They have an understanding of where they are in regards to where they want to be in relation to their career.

People who possess a low achievement striving score are people who are content with doing the bare minimum to just 'get by'. They lack the motivation and ambition to become successful and therefore often come across as lazy and have no direction as to where they want their careers to head.

These 30 questions will measure your level of achievement striving and help to determine your level of conscientiousness. The questions are simple; circle true or false to the statements provided and then use your answers to check your score.

Note: Reversed means that answering 'true' to the question will result in a low score of that trait.

1. I have ambitions in life.

True	False

2. I know how I want my life to go.

True	False

3. I know what I want and I go for it.

True	False

4. I am unsure about what I want from life. (Reversed)

True	False

5. My career is high on my priority list.

True	False

6. I aim to be successful in my chosen profession.

True	False

7. I want to work my way up to my ideal job.

True	False

8. I am an optimistic person.

True	False

9. My career is very important to me.

True	False

10. If you want something badly, you have to go for it.

True	False

11. I am highly driven to succeed.

True	False

12. I know what I want and I know how to get it.

True	False

13. People who have ambition only end up disappointed. (Reversed)

True	False

14. I won't let anyone get in the way of my dreams.

True	False

15. My career is the most important part in my life.

True	False

16. I set myself goals and targets every day.

True	False

17. I want to advance to the highest position in my chosen career.

True	False

18. My career is part of who I am.

True	False

19. If I had the chance, I wouldn't work at all. (Reversed)

True	False

20. I don't set myself goals because I know I won't reach them. (Reversed)

True	False

21. I always do my upmost in the work I do.

True	False

22. I put little effort in my work. (Reversed)

True	False

23. Everyone needs to have ambition.

True	False

24. I have clear direction of where my life is headed.

True	False

25. I am jealous of other people's success.

True	False

26. I feel overwhelmed at the prospect of getting my perfect career.

True	False

27. I do the minimal work possible. (Reversed)

True	False

28. I plan out the next step in my career path.

True	False

29. One step back only makes me more determined to succeed.

True	False

30. I consider myself as career orientated. My job is my life.

True	False

Scoring System:

Circle the letter that represents your chosen answer:

Note: make sure you circle the opposite answer from your above answer for the
Reversed answers

1.	T / F	2.	T / F	3.	T / F	4. (R)	T / F	5.	T / F
6.	T / F	7.	T / F	8.	T / F	9.	T / F	10.	T / F
11.	T / F	12.	T / F	13. (R)	T / F	14.	T / F	15.	T / F
16.	T / F	17.	T / F	18.	T / F	19. (R)	T / F	20. (R)	T / F
21.	T / F	22. (R)	T / F	23.	T / F	24.	T / F	25.	T / F
26.	T / F	27. (R)	T / F	28.	T / F	29.	T / F	30.	T / F

SCORE TOTAL:	True = ...	HIGH
SCORE TOTAL:	False = ...	LOW

Understanding Your Scores:

Your results on the achievement striving test will help determine your overall outcome for the trait of Conscientiousness. Once you've added up how many questions you answered true to, and how many questions you answered false, it will be a clear way of distinguishing if your score was high, average or low.

If you answered true to most of the questions, then below is a detailed explanation of what this means. If you answered false to most questions, then read the description for what a low response means. An average score considers both low and high traits, so therefore you should read that description.

HIGH (mostly true)	If you scored mostly true in the achievement striving test it means you show high levels of aspiration. You are an ambitious person who continually works hard in order to achieve your goals and ambition in life. You do your upmost to provide great quality of work and are not put off by the thoughts of challenge and hard work. Your career is your top priority. You value your profession and have goals for the future. You like to excel in your performance to better yourself. Employers value people who show ambition and dedication to their job. Generally, having ambition reinforces your interest and motivation within your chosen career which can be seen by employers. However, showing extreme levels of ambition may be a negative thing as this might suggest that you'll be looking for a higher position quickly. You need to be able to show your levels of ambition and enthusiasm, whilst still remaining happy and content with your current job.
AVERAGE	An average score means that whilst you do strive for achievement and success, you do not think about it too much and take it in its stride. You are an ambitious person. You want to succeed and do well and accomplish your aims and goals in life. You are a hard worker who values their career. Although you may not put 100% in everything you do, you work hard at most things. Sometimes you may show lack of motivation, but once you get going you put your best efforts into you work and hope for success.

LOW (mostly false)	If you scored mostly false in the achievement striving test, this demonstrates that you lack ambition, enthusiasm and motivation. You're the type of person who does just enough work to get them by. You don't go that extra mile in the work you do. You're simply content with a laid back approach and doing minimal work when possible. A very low score on striving for achievement often suggests lack of motivation. You have little direction in your work lifestyle and therefore find it difficult to show enthusiasm. You may show lack of enthusiasm because you haven't found the right job, or that your uncertain where to go next. This might influence your work ethic by not knowing what you want to achieve and how you want to achieve it. Employers want to see people that show interest, enthusiasm and ambition because it demonstrates a workforce that is committed and motivated. Try to aim for an average score that will enable you to put across your goals and ambition for your career in order to show motivation and enthusiasm. Even if you are not 100% sure of what your ambition maybe, you need to display that you are committed to your job role.

How Conscientious Are You?

So, you've finished answering all the questions on Conscientiousness. We have provided the table below to generate a general understanding of your level of conscientiousness.

Now go back through the six sub-traits for Conscientiousness and use your high, average and low scores to fill in the table below.

TRAIT	Compe-tence	Order	Dutiful-ness	Self-Disci-pline	Delibera-tion	Achievement Striving
HIGH, AVERAGE OR LOW?						

What does this mean overall?

HIGH	Conscientiousness refers to the social control a person possesses in terms of organising, planning and carrying out tasks.
	It is the ability to control your impulses and act on purposeful and effective ideas that have been thoroughly thought out and carefully deliberated.
	Your work ethic comes across as highly motivated and extremely ambitious. Your work performance excels and you do your upmost to get a job done from beginning to completion.
	You're the type of person who is often associated with academic and occupation achievement. In other words, you strive for excellence; you strive for success; you strive for yourself.
	You show vigilance and cautiousness that is often admired in a work place. You are reliable, efficient and independent. You get on with your job to the best of your ability without any distraction or procrastination.
	TRAITS = efficiency, ambitious, self-disciplined, resourceful, determined, strong willed

AVERAGE	An average score for conscientiousness means that you are a motivated person, with career orientated goals and ambition for success. You borderline both the high and low boundaries for both high and low scores which means that you possess characteristics from both. Generally, you are considered as a hardworking, motivated and ambitious person who strives for success. Although you may not give 100% in everything you do, you often try your hardest in your work. You occasionally act on impulse and don't think things through. However, you are often cautious and aware of the possible consequences that may lie ahead. Employers like to see a slightly high average score for conscientiousness. You want to demonstrate that you are reliable and hardworking who is willing to put effort and time into your work. **TRAITS = efficient, hardworking, motivated, impulsive, spontaneous, careless**
LOW	A lack of conscientiousness demonstrates your inability to be fully effective or reliable. Your struggle to think things through. You make quick and hasty decisions without any thought of the possible consequences. You act purely on impulse; whilst this generates quick responses and allows for direct and snap decisions, it can lead to carelessness and therefore diminishes a person's effectiveness. Unconscientious people are often criticised for their lack of motivation, unreliability and failure to comply with the rules and demands of the job. Other traits that are often associated with unconscientious are spontaneity, immaturity and impulsivity. They are not regarded as efficient workers and make it difficult to create a comfortable and competent working environment. **TRAITS = impulsive, careless, hasty, immature, unorganised, demotivated, spontaneous**

What does this say to employers about your personality?

People who are willing to take order and follow instruction and demonstrate a genuine interest in their job are people who are extremely valued by their employers. Hard work and deliberation doesn't go unnoticed by employers and it demonstrates high levels of interest.

The potential for progression in a workplace is often desired. Employers like to see people who want to progress further in the company. Striving for achievement and showing ambition is highly noticeable in a workplace. People who generate a clear sign for conscientiousness are people who are willing to do whatever it takes to do their best, become the best and someday, achieve their best.

CHAPTER 5 - The Big 5:

Openness

CHAPTER 5 - THE BIG 5: OPENNESS

The Big 5 model of personality also categorises people in regards to openness. Openness refers to an individual's ability to be open to experiences. Openness to experience describes the dimensions of cognitive styles that illuminate people who can be characterised by their imagination and creativity. Open people appreciate art and literature. They are fixated with this idea of beauty and fantasy.

Other elements that reinforce openness are active and vivid imaginations, attentiveness, intellectual curiosity and independent of judgements. They experience both positive and negative emotions and often show curious behaviour in relation to both the inner and outer worlds.

People who tend to be less open display more traditional and conservative views of life. They prefer familiarity. Low scorers tend to have narrow minded and common interests. They prefer the straightforward approach that is direct and obvious. These people tend to be traditionalists in regards to their feelings and are frequently resistant to change.

The term openness is often presented as healthier and mature in psychological studies as they too tend to be open minded. However, depending on the requirements of the situation and the job role you are applying for, depends how much openness is valued and desired. This test will give you some indication to what level of openness you possess and how it is perceived as both a positive and negative.

There are several sub-traits that personality tests look at to measure openness. These indicate psychological states of mind which are often analysed in terms of **fantasy, aesthetics, feelings, actions, ideas and values.**

In this chapter, it will focus on each one of these terms and assess your personality to determine your level of openness.

FANTASY

The Big 5 model of personality assesses many personality traits in order to gain an overview of a candidate's persona. One of the key elements that is analysed in personality tests is this idea of fantasy. The term fantasy refers to imagination. In psychology, these people are said to have vivid imaginations and divergent thinking. Openness to fantasies suggests an active imagination that demonstrates high levels of creativity. Daydreams and fantasies are used by people to create interesting scenarios and provide an escape route from their everyday lives.

People who score highly for fantasy possess characteristics such as creativity, active imaginations and curiosity. They tend to be people who are daydreamers and therefore create fantasy scenarios in order to distract themselves from reality. They see everyday life as plain, traditional and ordinary, and so, fantasies create the illusion of something more interesting.

People who score low on the scale of fantasy are set in their ways. Low scorers like to be fact based rather than make believe. They like to be practical rather than irrational. They like to be assured of stability, tradition and routine.

These 30 questions will measure your level of fantasy and help to determine your level of openness. The questions are simple; circle true or false to the statements provided and then use your answers to check your score.

Note: Reversed means that answering 'true' to the question
will result in a high score of that trait.

1. I enjoy daydreaming. (Reversed)

True	False

2. Seldom, I let my thoughts wander.

True	False

3. I consider myself a practical person.

True	False

4. I don't believe in make belief.

True	False

5. Fantasies are immature.

True	False

6. I have a vivid imagination. (Reversed)

| True | False |

7. I have a traditional way of life.

| True | False |

8. I like routine and structure.

| True | False |

9. I am creative. (Reversed)

| True | False |

10. I don't believe in fairy tales.

| True | False |

11. I don't often dive into fantasies.

| True | False |

12. I have difficulty imagining other alternatives.

| True | False |

13. I waste my time daydreaming. (Reversed)

| True | False |

14. I consider myself a realist.

| True | False |

15. Fantasists are not living realistically.

| True | False |

16. I am more interested in fact than fantasy.

| True | False |

17. I rarely experiment with life experiences.

| True | False |

18. I don't possess much of a creative imagination.

| True | False |

19. I would consider myself a conservative person.

True	False

20. I am not preoccupied by arts and fiction.

True	False

21. I get annoyed when other people get distracted and 'drift off'.

True	False

22. If I am at my desk, my mind is usually on my work.

True	False

23. I am always practical.

True	False

24. Sometimes, I daydream without even meaning to. (Reversed)

True	False

25. Fantasies show lack of life experiences.

True	False

26. Nothing good can come out of fantasising.

True	False

27. Sometimes I need an escape route from real life. (Reversed)

True	False

28. I am set in my ways.

True	False

29. I dislike change.

True	False

30. I often create illusions of possible scenarios. (Reversed)

True	False

Scoring System:

Circle the letter that represents your chosen answer:

Note: make sure you circle the opposite answer from your above answer for the Reversed answers

1. (R)	T / F	**2.**	T / F	**3.**	T / F	**4.**	T / F	**5.**	T / F
6. (R)	T / F	**7.**	T / F	**8.**	T / F	**9.** (R)	T / F	**10.**	T / F
11.	T / F	**12.**	T / F	**13.** (R)	T / F	**14.**	T / F	**15.**	T / F
16.	T / F	**17.**	T / F	**18.**	T / F	**19.**	T / F	**20.**	T / F
21.	T / F	**22.**	T / F	**23.**	T / F	**24.** (R)	T / F	**25.**	T / F
26.	T / F	**27.** (R)	T / F	**28.**	T / F	**29.**	T / F	**30.** (R)	T / F

SCORE TOTAL:	True =	....	LOW
SCORE TOTAL:	False =	....	HIGH

Understanding Your Scores:

Your results on the fantasy test will help determine your overall outcome for the trait of Openness. Once you've added up how many questions you answered true to, and how many questions you answered false, it will be a clear way of distinguishing if your score was high, average or low.

If you answered true to most of the questions, then below is a detailed explanation of what this means. If you answered false to most questions, then read the description for what a low response means. An average score considers both low and high traits, so therefore you should read that description.

HIGH (mostly false)	If you scored mostly false in the fantasy test it means you are considered a fantasist. You believe in using your creativity and imagination to create illusions and daydreams. You think the real world is ordinary and plain and thus you make up scenarios and 'drift off' into your own little world. You are the type of person who uses daydreams to provide an escape route from reality. It provides you with a sense of hope, peace and idealism that might not be found in your everyday lifestyle. You find routine and structure boring. You are easily distracted and often find your mind on others things than your work. You want to aim for a low score in relation to fantasy. No one wants to employ people who are constantly day dreaming and 'drift off'. You do not want to be perceived as immature and impractical.
AVERAGE	If you scored an average score for fantasy this means that you are prone to the occasional fantasy and distraction of imagination. Generally you are considered as someone who is focused and rarely finds their mind wandering away from the task. However, sometimes this does happen. You may get distracted and let your mind wander on other things, but you are able to quickly get back on track. You like facts but do enjoy the occasional fantasy and imaginative thinking. You like to use daydreams as an escape route but overall, you like to stay focused and stick to your daily routine.

LOW (mostly true)	If you scored mostly true in the fantasy test, this shows that you have low levels of fantasy and creative imagination. You lack the ability to use your imagination for anything other than your work. You rarely find your mind wandering on other things and you seldom get distracted by fantasies. You are the type of person who prefers fact and truth rather than fantasy and fiction. You like to keep their emotions muted to ensure that they are not distracted. You tend to be more set in your ways. You rarely wander from your everyday routine and find that you have a more conservative outlook on life. Employers like to be assured that their workforce is focused. No employer, no matter what position likes to see their employees constantly daydreaming and becoming distracted. They prefer people who have direction.

AESTHETICS

Another facet that underlies the important personality trait of openness is aesthetics. This refers to particular artistic interests a person may possess. People who believe in the importance of art have a deep appreciation for beauty, art and nature. They are somewhat moved and absorbed by these elements of the world which shows genuine interest into culture, natural surroundings and fine art.

People who score highly on the scale of aesthetics demonstrate all of the above. They show interests into the world around them and appreciates fine art and detail. They are emotionally moved by aesthetically pleasing and idealistic elements of the world in which they live.

People with a lack of interest in regards to aesthetics show little appreciation in terms of the arts. They lack sensitivity in relation to aesthetics and are not necessarily interested in the world around them. They don't enjoy fine art or literature or poetry.

These 30 questions will measure your level of aesthetics and artistic interests and help to determine your level of openness. The questions are simple; circle true or false to the statements provided and then use your answers to check your score.

**Note: Reversed means that answering 'true' to the question will result in a low score of that trait.**

1. I appreciate my surroundings.

| True | False |

2. I enjoy art museums.

| True | False |

3. I enjoy the finer details in life.

| True | False |

4. I find the countryside serene and aesthetically beautiful.

| True | False |

5. I wouldn't consider myself a massive lover of art. (Reversed)

| True | False |

6. I would be bored if I had to go out to look at sceneries. (Reversed)

| True | False |

7. I would consider myself a deep and soulful person.

True	False

8. I don't take much interest in the world around me. (Reversed)

True	False

9. I find it difficult to interact with the world around me. (Reversed)

True	False

10. I enjoy going for walks in the countryside.

True	False

11. I love nature.

True	False

12. Nothing beats a beautiful and scenic view.

True	False

13. I could look at landscapes and views for ages without being bored.

True	False

14. I would consider myself an intellectual person.

True	False

15. I am quite the art lover.

True	False

16. I like poetry.

True	False

17. I often stop to look at a view.

True	False

18. I am moved by beauty and art.

True	False

19. Art is an important part of culture.

True	False

20. I enjoy getting to grips with different cultures and sceneries.

| True | False |

21. I often seek places that are beautiful and quiet.

| True | False |

22. I like to experience deep, intense feelings.

| True | False |

23. I often watch the sunset.

| True | False |

24. I rarely take any notice of nature. (Reversed)

| True | False |

25. Nature is true beauty.

| True | False |

26. I love to interact with the world around me.

| True | False |

27. I often visit galleries and museums.

| True | False |

28. I appreciate a good painting.

| True | False |

29. I don't understand art. (Reversed)

| True | False |

30. Life would be boring without art, literature and nature.

| True | False |

Scoring System:

Circle the letter that represents your chosen answer:

Note: make sure you circle the opposite answer from your above answer for the Reversed answers

1. T / F	2. T / F	3. T / F	4. T / F	5. T / F (R)
6. T / F (R)	7. T / F	8. T / F (R)	9. T / F (R)	10. T / F
11. T / F	12. T / F	13. T / F	14. T / F	15. T / F
16. T / F	17. T / F	18. T / F	19. T / F	20. T / F
21. T / F	22. T / F	23. T / F	24. T / F (R)	25. T / F
26. T / F	27. T / F	28. T / F	29. T / F (R)	30. T / F

SCORE TOTAL:	True =	....	HIGH
SCORE TOTAL:	False =	....	LOW

Understanding Your Scores:

Your results on the aesthetics test will help determine your overall outcome for the trait of Openness. Once you've added up how many questions you answered true to, and how many questions you answered false, it will be a clear way of distinguishing if your score was high, average or low.

If you answered true to most of the questions, then below is a detailed explanation of what this means. If you answered false to most questions, then read the description for what a low response means. An average score considers both low and high traits, so therefore you should read that description.

HIGH (mostly true)	If you scored mostly true, it means that you are highly engaged with aesthetics and social surroundings. You appreciate the finer things in life. You take an artistic interest in art, literature and nature. You show deep gratitude and contentment for detail and beauty. You believe in the importance of art and beauty. Depending on the type of job role and traits required, depends on how much aesthetics and artistic interest you need to show. Some jobs require you to be able to show levels of fine detail and precision in the way something looks. This demonstrate your creative and artistic ability. However, some jobs do not require you to take an interest in art or literature, so you need to aim your score based on your chosen profession.
AVERAGE	An average score on aesthetics means that you do enjoy the finer things in life. You are sensitive and satisfied by beauty, art and literature, but you don't show a huge interest as someone with a higher score would. You are aware of literature, fine art, beauty and nature but you don't take huge amounts of time to stop and think about it. Depending on your chosen job profession, depends if you need to show levels of artistic interests. Obviously, if you were to work in something creative, you would need to show that you appreciate creative ideas and images. However, other jobs may not require you to take a general interest in aesthetics, so you should aim your score depending on the traits required.

LOW (mostly false)	If you scored mostly false, it means that you show lack of interest in regards to aesthetics and artistic wellbeing.

You don't take the time to stop and look at beautiful landscapes and you have no interest in art, museums or literature.

You lack sensitivity in regards to nature, culture and your social surroundings. You have little appreciation for them and don't acknowledge these elements of life as particularly significant.

You take no pride in gaining knowledge and satisfaction from the worlds of fine art and detail and therefore lack ability to engage with the social world. |

FEELINGS

Personality tests often focus on a person's feelings and emotions. Under the personality trait of openness, feelings is another facet that is often explored to demonstrate levels of emotionalism and sensitivity. The term feelings refers to an individual's reception to their own feelings and often experiences moments of emotionalism.

People who experience high levels of feelings and emotions believe it is an important element of life. Everyone gets emotional. It just depends how much a person shows it in terms of extremeness. They experience deep and differentiated feelings of mixed emotions and find it difficult to keep them bottled up.

People who experience low levels of feelings and emotions are rarely good at showing how they feel. They are less aware of their emotions and tend not to express their emotions openly. These people tend to be more reserved and independent. They are reluctant at showing their vulnerability.

These 30 questions will measure your level of feelings and emotions and help to determine your level of openness. The questions are simple; circle true or false to the statements provided and then use your answers to check your score.

Note: Reversed means that answering 'true' to the question will result in a low score of that trait.

1. I am a sensitive person.

True	False

2. I often express my emotions.

True	False

3. I am easily upset.

True	False

4. I tend to bottle up my feelings. (Reversed)

True	False

5. I consider myself an open person.

True	False

6. I often express how I am feeling.

True	False

7. If I am upset, people usually know.

True	False

8. I am not good at keeping my feelings to myself.

True	False

9. If I don't express my feelings, I will explode.

True	False

10. Everyone gets emotional and needs to just let it out.

True	False

11. Don't bring negative feelings to work. (Reversed)

True	False

12. I am a very private person. (Reversed)

True	False

13. I often get mad and upset.

True	False

14. I have a short fuse.

True	False

15. I keep my emotions in check. (Reversed)

True	False

16. I am not good at handling my emotions.

True	False

17. If I am upset, I have to tell somebody.

True	False

18. I can't control my feelings.

True	False

19. I get caught up in all my emotions.

True	False

20. I am an emotional person.

True	False

21. If someone shouts at me, I get upset.

True	False

22. I tend not to let my emotions interfere with my work. (Reversed)

True	False

23. I would feel self-conscious if I expressed my emotions at work. (Reversed)

True	False

24. I often cry.

True	False

25. I get upset over the smallest things.

True	False

26. I find it difficult to voice my feelings. (Reversed)

True	False

27. I am the emotional person in my group of friends.

True	False

28. I don't like people seeing me upset. (Reversed)

True	False

29. I feel better after I express my feelings.

True	False

30. I often feel in a vulnerable state.

True	False

Scoring System:

Circle the letter that represents your chosen answer:

Note: make sure you circle the opposite answer from your above answer for the Reversed answers

1. T / F	**2.** T / F	**3.** T / F	**4.** (R) T / F	**5.** T / F
6. T / F	**7.** T / F	**8.** T / F	**9.** T / F	**10.** T / F
11. (R) T / F	**12.** (R) T / F	**13.** T / F	**14.** T / F	**15.** (R) T / F
16. T / F	**17.** T / F	**18.** T / F	**19.** T / F	**20.** T / F
21. T / F	**22.** (R) T / F	**23.** (R) T / F	**24.** T / F	**25.** T / F
26. (R) T / F	**27.** T / F	**28.** (R) T / F	**29.** T / F	**30.** T / F

SCORE TOTAL:	True =	....	HIGH
SCORE TOTAL:	False =	....	LOW

Understanding Your Scores:

Your results on the feelings and emotions test will help determine your overall outcome for the trait of Openness. Once you've added up how many questions you answered true to, and how many questions you answered false, it will be a clear way of distinguishing if your score was high, average or low.

If you answered true to most of the questions, then below is a detailed explanation of what this means. If you answered false to most questions, then read the description for what a low response means. An average score considers both low and high traits, so therefore you should read that description.

HIGH (mostly true)	If you scored mostly true, you show extreme high levels of feelings and emotionalism. You are an extremely open person. You don't mind sharing your feelings and expressing how you feel. You struggle to bottle up your feelings and keeping your emotions to yourself. You are an extremely sensitive and emotional person who has good access to and awareness of their own feelings. You experience deep and emotional states of mind. You believe it is important to share your feelings and often explore your sensitive side. Employers don't want to employ people who are continuously upset or getting emotional. However, showing no emotion whatsoever shows lack of compassion and interest. You want to aim for a score which borders both the high and low scale of emotionalism. You want to be able to show your passionate and sensitive side towards certain issues, but also show you're able to constrain your feelings and not let it affect your work.
AVERAGE	An average score for feelings and emotions means that you show a great balance between holding back your emotions and letting them go. You are an open person who likes to express their emotions. You are a sensitive person but not overly sensitive. Although you express your feelings when a situation plays on your mind or you have something to say, you try to keep yourself to yourself. You try not to let your emotional state get in the way at work, but sometimes it cannot be helped. You are the type of person who is able to restrain themselves from emotional turmoil if a situation does not require you to get overly involved, however you have no apprehension of expressing your views if something upsets you or if you are presented with something you don't agree with.

LOW (mostly false)	If you scored mostly false, you show extreme low levels of expressing your feelings and emotions. You are an extremely reserved person. You keep yourself to yourself and rarely show your emotional state of mind. Low scorers tend not to express their feelings and are generally more conservative and private people. You don't like the idea of vulnerability. Showing emotions puts you an extremely vulnerable position. You try to avoid this feeling as it creates a sense of lack of self-esteem and confidence. Employers like to be able to see that their employees are capable of keeping their emotions to themselves. Employers like to know that feelings won't get in the way of your work. The common saying of keeping your private life at home is often implied for many businesses. Businesses want to ensure employees are effective and strong-minded and who are not easily distracted. Employers also like employees who don't often get upset, and keep a focused mind-set.

ACTIONS

A person's actions are another way in which openness is explored. Actions explores the willingness to try new and different activities. These people who display high levels of action tend to be referred to as adventurous. Adventurous people are eager to experience change. They like to be able to take routine and make it 'different'.

People who experience high levels of adventurousness, are generally considered as ambitious, active and venturous. They find routine and structure boring, and therefore like to experience change and different alternatives.

People who experience lack of action are people who do not take change well. They like the security and stability of routine and structure. They like to feel familiar with something. They are not people who stray from their familiar routine. They are not considered as adventurous.

These 30 questions will measure your level of actions and adventurousness and help to determine your level of openness. The questions are simple; circle true or false to the statements provided and then use your answers to check your score.

Note: Reversed means that answering 'true' to the question will result in a low score of that trait.

1.   I often seek variety.

True	False

2.   I like to experience new things.

True	False

3.   I find routine boring.

True	False

4.   I consider myself an adventurous person.

True	False

5.   I like to stick to what I know. (Reversed)

True	False

6.   I am happy to try things I've never tried before.

True	False

7. I enjoy taking a little risk.

| True | False |

8. I prefer to stick to routine. (Reversed)

| True | False |

9. I don't like the idea of being audacious. (Reversed)

| True | False |

10. I don't like the idea of experimentation. (Reversed)

| True | False |

11. I don't mind change.

| True | False |

12. I go with the flow; I don't have a routine.

| True | False |

13. I get bored easily with routine.

| True | False |

14. If someone asked me to do something daring, I would usually do it.

| True | False |

15. I am a conservative person. (Reversed)

| True | False |

16. I like knowing that I am good at something I do all the time. (Reversed)

| True | False |

17. Live everyday like it's your last, take a risk!

| True | False |

18. I feel uncomfortable with the unfamiliar. (Reversed)

| True | False |

19. My actions are usually active.

| True | False |

20. I am always audacious.

True	False

21. I am always bored with familiarity.

True	False

22. I seek novelty and variety.

True	False

23. I am not a cautious person.

True	False

24. I am often curious.

True	False

25. I travel to different places every time I go on holiday.

True	False

26. I think it's pointless to go on holiday to a place you've been before.

True	False

27. I feel uneasy if I don't know where I am. (Reversed)

True	False

28. I like experimentation.

True	False

29. I would consider myself as venturous.

True	False

30. I like security and stability. (Reversed)

True	False

Scoring System:

Circle the letter that represents your chosen answer:

Note: make sure you circle the opposite answer from your above answer for the Reversed answers

1. T / F	**2.** T / F	**3.** T / F	**4.** T / F	**5.** T / F (R)
6. T / F	**7.** T / F	**8.** T / F (R)	**9.** T / F (R)	**10.** T / F (R)
11. T / F	**12.** T / F	**13.** T / F	**14.** T / F	**15.** T / F (R)
16. T / F (R)	**17.** T / F	**18.** T / F (R)	**19.** T / F	**20.** T / F
21. T / F	**22.** T / F	**23.** T / F	**24.** T / F	**25.** T / F
26. T / F	**27.** T / F (R)	**28.** T / F	**29.** T / F	**30.** T / F (R)

SCORE TOTAL:	True =	....	HIGH
SCORE TOTAL:	False =	....	LOW

Understanding Your Scores:

Your results on the actions and adventurous test will help determine your overall outcome for the trait of Openness. Once you've added up how many questions you answered true to, and how many questions you answered false, it will be a clear way of distinguishing if your score was high, average or low.

If you answered true to most of the questions, then below is a detailed explanation of what this means. If you answered false to most questions, then read the description for what a low response means. An average score considers both low and high traits, so therefore you should read that description.

HIGH (mostly true)	If you scored mostly true, this means you score extreme high levels for actions and adventurousness. Adventurous people like experimentation. They like to try different things, experience alternative ways and are eager for change. You are extremely venturous, curious, eager and open to new experiences. You tend to find daily routine and familiarity tedious and tiring. People who experience high levels of venture and action can be assessed in terms of positivity and negativity. Employers like to see people who are open to change and new ideas which show initiative, broadmindedness and flexibility. However, extreme high scores might suggest your inability to show cautiousness and therefore you may be prone to impulsive behaviour. You need to show a balance of level of action and adventurousness. Depending on your job role and the traits required, you need to show some levels of action and the ability to show flexibility, forward thinking and openness to change.
AVERAGE	Showing a balance of caution and deliberation, as well as the ability to be flexible and somewhat adventurous is important. You want to be able to demonstrate you're capable of experiencing both adventures and routine. You are curious and open to new experiences. However, you do like your routine and knowing what you are doing on a certain day at a certain time. You are adaptable of stepping outside your comfort zone and experiencing something venturous and different.

LOW (mostly false)	If you scored mostly false on the test for actions and adventurousness, this means you demonstrate extreme low levels of ability to venture out and be active. Unlike adventurous people who live more carefree and risky, you are more inclined to show caution and deliberation. You are uncomfortable with change. You feel uneasy when you are presented with new ideas of alternative approaches to your usual routine. You prefer routine. You like to follow structure and have clear direction. You find it difficult to accept something different and therefore show your lack of flexibility. Try not to score such an extreme low score. Employers do not want to employ people who show that they are unable to follow change or are unable to try a different way.

IDEAS

Openness is also measured by looking at an individual's **ideas** and intellectual ability. Ideas and intellect demonstrate willingness to pursue complex ideas and engage with philosophical and theoretical debates. They have an intellectual curiosity that enables them to willingly try new ideas. Intellectual people tend to be open-minded. A key thing to remember when dealing with ideas and intellectual ability, is that it doesn't assess a person's intelligence. It assesses a person's ideas and style rather than intellectual ability.

People who possess high scores for intellectual style are people who enjoy complex issues and get involved with controversial theories and ideas. They are open to new ideas and enjoy experimenting with them. They enjoy complex issues such as brain teasers and riddles, which often provides them with stimulation and motivation.

Low scorers of intellectual ideas avoid philosophical and complex discussions. These people often display themselves as more of a people person than an idea person. They believe intellectual ideas are a waste of time.

These 30 questions will measure your level of intellectual style and ideas and help to determine your level of openness. The questions are simple; circle true or false to the statements provided and then use your answers to check your score.

Note: Reversed means that answering 'true' to the question will result in a low score of that trait.

1. I often enjoy thinking about theories and concepts.

   | True | False |

2. I like to engage with complex and abstract ideas.

   | True | False |

3. I often read difficult reading material.

   | True | False |

4. I can handle lots of new and complex information.

   | True | False |

5. My vocabulary is very limited. (Reversed)

   | True | False |

6. I like experimenting with different ideas.

True	False

7. I often like to try new experiences.

True	False

8. I would consider myself an intellect.

True	False

9. I find it difficult to understand complex information. (Reversed)

True	False

10. I like brain teasers, puzzles and riddles.

True	False

11. I get easily frustrated if I cannot work something out. (Reversed)

True	False

12. I try to gain a deep and thorough understanding in regards to my work.

True	False

13. I like to be given lots of information to work on something.

True	False

14. I get involved with complex discussions.

True	False

15. I am interested in discussions that become theoretical.

True	False

16. I seldom do extra research on my work. (Reversed)

True	False

17. I think philosophical arguments are tedious. (Reversed)

True	False

18. My friends and I often get into theoretical debate.

True	False

19. I like to take a different approach on similar situations.

| True | False |

20. I always try something new.

| True | False |

21. My friends often consider me as the knowledgeable one of the group.

| True | False |

22. I try to use a wide vocabulary.

| True | False |

23. I like doing research.

| True | False |

24. I like engaging with meaningful conversations.

| True | False |

25. If something is unclear, I would do my research.

| True | False |

26. I am not interested in theory or debate. (Reversed)

| True | False |

27. I prefer quick decision making rather than careful deliberations. (Reversed)

| True | False |

28. I enjoy reading up about things.

| True | False |

29. I tend to avoid topics that are deep and abstract. (Reversed)

| True | False |

30. I believe that I have great intellect ability and am willing to try new things.

| True | False |

Scoring System:

Circle the letter that represents your chosen answer:

Note: make sure you circle the opposite answer from your above answer for the Reversed answers

1.	T / F	2.	T / F	3.	T / F	4.	T / F	5. (R)	T / F
6.	T / F	7.	T / F	8.	T / F	9. (R)	T / F	10.	T / F
11. (R)	T / F	12.	T / F	13.	T / F	14.	T / F	15.	T / F
16. (R)	T / F	17. (R)	T / F	18.	T / F	19.	T / F	20.	T / F
21.	T / F	22.	T / F	23.	T / F	24.	T / F	25.	T / F
26. (R)	T / F	27. (R)	T / F	28.	T / F	29. (R)	T / F	30.	T / F

SCORE TOTAL:	True =	....	HIGH
SCORE TOTAL:	False =	....	LOW

Understanding Your Scores:

Your results on the ideas and intellect test will help determine your overall outcome for the trait of Openness. Once you've added up how many questions you answered true to, and how many questions you answered false, it will be a clear way of distinguishing if your score was high, average or low.

If you answered true to most of the questions, then below is a detailed explanation of what this means. If you answered false to most questions, then read the description for what a low response means. An average score considers both low and high traits, so therefore you should read that description.

HIGH (mostly true)	If you scored mostly true, this means that you show high levels of ideas and intellectual ability.

You have intellectual curiosity and are keen to pursue ideas regarding philosophical and theoretical debates.

You are considered as thorough, enthusiastic, and knowledgeable in regards to your approach and style.

Depending on the job position you have; it depends how much of your own ideas intellectual you want to convey. Professional roles, senior management and IT jobs require the ability to show high levels of intellectual ability and ideas.

However, some jobs do not require your intellectual ability and ideas and thus, prefer less intellect if your job doesn't require it in order to maintain stimulation and have less chance of becoming bored. |
| **AVERAGE** | An average score for ideas and intellect means that you sometimes show the ability to engage with theoretical and philosophical debates.

You are not overly keep on theory or debate, but you are capable of putting your views across and demonstrating your knowledge and understanding of a particular subject matter.

However, you also like to deal with people as opposed to theory. You are adaptable at showing interests in interacting with people or interacting with information and data.

Employers like to see some levels of ideas and intellectual ability but it really depends on the type of role you are applying for. Some jobs will require you to show more ideas and intellect than others. |

LOW (mostly false)	If you score mostly false, this demonstrates that you show low levels of ideas and intellect. You tend to be less concerned with engaging in philosophical and theoretical debate. You prefer dealing with people rather than complex and ideas. Some employers will assess your ability to demonstrate your ideas and intellect based on the job role you are applying for. Some jobs require you to be able to show some levels or intellectual style and engage with difficult and challenging theory and knowledge. However, some jobs are concerned with conducting a more fast-paced working environment and therefore require quick decision making skills as opposed to intellectual ability.

VALUES

In order to assess one's openness, the term **values** is often analysed to determine significant personality traits. Personality tests analyses values in order to determine a person's thought and belief process in regards to social, political and religious elements of the world.

Values is often associated with this notion of liberalism. It assesses a person's ability to show readiness and challenge authority, convention and tradition. High scorers of such values tend to vote for liberals to explore a philosophical approach to gain equality and liberty. They can often represent hostile views towards rules and regulations and are sympathetic to rule-breakers. They enjoy the ideas of chaos and disruption.

Low scorers in relation to values believe in one true tradition. They prefer the stability and comfort in which tradition and rules brings to their lifestyles. They are often conformists. Closed individuals are often those who accept authority and don't challenge existing hierarchies, structures or ideologies. They simply are dogmatic and honour tradition.

These 30 questions will measure your level of values and help to determine your level of openness. The questions are simple; circle true or false to the statements provided and then use your answers to check your score.

Note: Reversed means that answering 'true' to the question will result in a low score of that trait.

1. I consider myself an eccentric person.

True	False

2. I often express my thoughts and feelings on important issues.

True	False

3. I like to challenge authority.

True	False

4. If I don't agree with something, I will challenge it.

True	False

5. I am a conformist. (Reversed)

True	False

6. I often break tradition.

| True | False |

7. Stability and security is tedious.

| True | False |

8. I find tradition boring.

| True | False |

9. I am empathetic to rule breakers.

| True | False |

10. I tend not to follow authority.

| True | False |

11. I like to do my own thing.

| True | False |

12. I do not change my beliefs because someone says they're wrong.

| True | False |

13. I find rules and regulations extremely limiting.

| True | False |

14. I often deviate from convention.

| True | False |

15. I am not a rule breaker. (Reversed)

| True | False |

16. I don't question authority. (Reversed)

| True | False |

17. I like to start new traditions.

| True | False |

18. Hierarchy is there for a reason. (Reversed)

| True | False |

19. Tradition is not always best.

True	False

20. I enjoy chaos and disorder.

True	False

21. I consider myself ambiguous.

True	False

22. I prefer stability and security. (Reversed)

True	False

23. I show hostility towards things I don't agree with.

True	False

24. I like to voice my opinions.

True	False

25. I don't like to feel supressed and manipulated.

True	False

26. Hierarchy takes no consideration of everyone's thoughts and feelings.

True	False

27. I rarely follow what everyone else is doing.

True	False

28. The freedom to do and say what I want is very important to me.

True	False

29. I usually adapt my behaviour to fit in. (Reversed)

True	False

30. I would never stray away from my values and beliefs, despite going against authority.

True	False

Scoring System:

Circle the letter that represents your chosen answer:

Note: make sure you circle the opposite answer from your above answer for the Reversed answers

1. T / F	2. T / F	3. T / F	4. T / F	5. T / F (R)
6. T / F	7. T / F	8. T / F	9. T / F	10. T / F
11. T / F	12. T / F	13. T / F	14. T / F	15. T / F (R)
16. T / F (R)	17. T / F	18. T / F (R)	19. T / F	20. T / F
21. T / F	22. T / F (R)	23. T / F	24. T / F	25. T / F
26. T / F	27. T / F	28. T / F	29. T / F (R)	30. T / F

SCORE TOTAL:	True =	....	HIGH
SCORE TOTAL:	False =	....	LOW

Understanding Your Scores:

Your results on the values test will help determine your overall outcome for the trait of Openness. Once you've added up how many questions you answered true to, and how many questions you answered false, it will be a clear way of distinguishing if your score was high, average or low.

If you answered true to most of the questions, then below is a detailed explanation of what this means. If you answered false to most questions, then read the description for what a low response means. An average score considers both low and high traits, so therefore you should read that description.

HIGH (mostly true)	If you scored mostly true in the values test, this means that you show high levels of values. Your personality demonstrates that you take a liberal approach. This doesn't mean that you support liberalism or have any acknowledgment in political affiliation; it just means to say that your mind-set takes on a liberal approach. Psychological liberalism suggests that you often challenge authority and tradition. You like to re-assess social, political and religious values. You are somewhat rebellious and enjoy ambiguity and disorder. You like to be able to express your feelings and values, and feel like you have a voice in the subject matter. You do not like to feel repressed and manipulated by social hierarchies. Employers like to see that you are able to express your thoughts and ideas. They like to see that people are able to show levels of independent thinking and are not manipulated. However, showing extreme high levels might indicate that you are rebellious and unable to conform to the rules and regulations of the working environment.
AVERAGE	An average score in the values test means you border the high and low scale. You are able to demonstrate a versatile and flexible approach in regards to expressing your values. Employers like to see that you can follow tradition and conform to the rules and regulations that you are provided with. As an employee, you will be given instructions and rules to follow which you should comply with. However, you are the type of person who will reject instructions or rules based on personal beliefs or values or if you disagree with them. You like to be given the opportunity to express your feelings and values regarding a particular matter and for your voice to be heard and taken into consideration. You are the type of person that often follows the rules and are able to comply with what is asked of them, but are not afraid to stand up for what they believe in and voice their concerns when the time comes.

LOW (mostly false)	If you scored mostly false in the values test, this suggests that you show low levels of values and are therefore more conservative. You like structure. You are a conformist and always follow the rules and regulations that are set for you. You do not challenge and you do not argue. You tend not to make your own traditions and therefore you often follow tradition. You often keep your feelings and values bottled up in order to provide a comfortable and calm working environment. Although employers like to see their employees are capable of complying with the rules and regulations of the company, they also want to see that you are capable of thinking for yourself. You need to show that you have your own beliefs and thoughts and are therefore able to voice these when it is required.

How Open Are You?

So, you've finished answering all the questions on Openness. We have provided the table below to generate a general understanding of your level of openness.

Now go back through the six sub-traits for Openness and use your high, average and low scores to fill in the table below'

TRAIT	Fantasy	Aesthetics	Feelings	Actions	Ideas	Values
HIGH, AVERAGE OR LOW?						

What does this mean overall?

HIGH	Individuals that possess a high level of openness show willingness to different life experiences. They like experiencing different things and acknowledge the smaller things in life. They enjoy all things compromising of beauty, art, and fantasies.
	You are considered imaginative. Your imagination tends to run wild and paint up vivid scenarios. This demonstrates that you have a creative and artistic ability and enjoy artistic interests such as art, nature and social surroundings.
	You are the type of person who is full of life and are adventurous. You like to experience new things to keep life interesting.
	You are full of ideas and values that are very important to you. These ideologies and beliefs make up the person you are and you like to be able to share these with other people.
	High scorers for openness often challenge authority and tradition. They like to be able to put their mark on an important subject. They like to be able to voice their opinions.
	TRAITS = imaginative, open, expressive, curious, enthusiastic, independent, original

AVERAGE	People with an average score of openness shows the ability to show openness and resilience. You are the type of person who not only likes taking adventures and experiencing new things, but you also like to feel secure and stable through routine and structure. You have ideas and values that you like to express. Although you can conform to the rules and regulations set by the company, you are not afraid to voice your opinion and stand up for yourself. Although you like to contribute to a calm and comfortable working environment, by voicing your concerns and disagreeing with the rules, this could lead to a hostile and slightly awkward work place. **TRAITS = expressive, curious, enthusiastic, cautious, conventional, reserved** Employers like to see employees who are open to new ideas and experiences and follow command, but also have the confidence to express their views and come up with ideas for themselves.
LOW	People that score a low score on the openness are extremely reserved and conservative people. Those who score low on openness are extremely conventional and high on tradition. You never stray away from the rules and regulations that are set and therefore never challenge authority. You like to be assured of security and stability. You believe it is important to have a realistic understanding of the world we live in and therefore have a clear and direct mind set. You don't fantasise or indulge in 'what ifs'. You like routine and structure. You tend to keep your feelings and beliefs very close to your chest. You don't like to feel vulnerable by expressing yourself, so you tend to be more withdrawn. You know what you want and you know exactly how to get it. You do what it takes to achieve your goals without deviating from convention. **TRAITS = cautious, mild, conservative, reserved, conformist, conventional**

What does this say to employers about your personality?

A person who is open and expressive is a person that shows their capabilities of independence and creative mind set. Employers want to see a fine balance between being open and being reserved. Employers like to see that individuals are capable of thinking out loud, that they can voice their opinion and express any ideas and thoughts that they may have.

However, they also like to see individuals who can conform to existing traditions and rules and show willingness to strive and succeed. Employers prefer employees who are able to keep your personal life at home and maintain a healthy work ethic. Depending on your job role, will depend on the level of openness you want to convey.

CHAPTER 6

Traits Required
For Specific Job Positions

CHAPTER 6
TRAITS REQUIRED FOR SPECIFIC JOB POSITIONS

Your results from the tests in the previous chapters should provide you with a clear indication of the particular personality traits that you possess.

You are now able to take those traits and determine if they are desirable in your chosen job. This is likely to assess your success rate and whether you would be suitable for the job role.

The table below is specifically designed to enable you to use your scores on personality traits to assess whether they are relevant and desirable to the job position that you are applying for.

Now go back through each chapter and using the final table in each chapter (i.e. the tables that show how neurotic, open you are etc), and use those key traits to determine what jobs find those traits desirable or not.

POSTION	DESIRABLE/ UNDESIR- ABLE	TRAITS
All positions	High	Perseverance, adaptable, conscientious, optimistic, aware
	Low	Vulnerable, daydreamer, apprehensive, hostile
Senior manage- ment	High	Dominant, resilient, assertive, creative, impulsive, inde- pendent, critical thinker, self-disciplined, active, ambitious
	Low	Vulnerable, unmotivated, self-conscious, empathetic, conservative
Middle Manager	High	Dominant, organised, assertive, competitive, active, ambi- tious, creative
	Low	Vulnerable, self-conscious, day-dreamer, humble
Junior manage- ment	High	Ambitious, compliant, assertive, active, dutiful, achieve- ment striving, dynamic, competitive, positive
	Low	Vulnerable, depressed, self-conscious, fantasist
Profess- ional	High	Critical thinker, compliant, self-disciplined, competent, independent, social comfort, intellectual ability
	Low	Vulnerable, hostile, self-conscious
Graduate	High	Ambitious, independent, compliant, altruistic, competent, self-disciplined, achievement striving
	Low	Vulnerable, unmotivated, day dreamer

Semi-skilled workers	High	Team player, trusting, compliant, assertive, order, competent
	Low	Dominant, direct, vulnerable, averted to routine
Sales	High	Sales and negotiation orientated, trusting, tender minded, positive, creative, empathetic, tolerant
	Low	Humble, vulnerable, daydreamer, hostile, conscious
IT / Engineer	High	Critical thinker, creative, intellectual ability, competent
	Low	Conservative, team player, companionship, vulnerable
Technical	High	Critical thinker, independent, competent
	Low	Averted to routine
Customer service	High	Tolerant, sales and negotiation orientated, empathetic, trusting, consulting ability, straightforward
	Low	Dominant, vulnerable, hostile, depressed, daydreamer, direct

Despite the controversy regarding personality tests, they are becoming increasingly popular in the selection process, so you must be able to identify your key strengths and weaknesses and answer the questions in accordance to what employers are looking for. These tests will help determine whether you are the right candidate for the job position and whether you hold the right personality traits which the employers are looking for.

Some people believe that personality tests are unreliable and inaccurate. Truth be it that these tests cannot gain a complete recognition of your personality nor can they guarantee and predict your future in relation to your career. But what they can do is pinpoint parts of your personality that you may have overlooked, and generate some indication of the type of characteristics in which you excel in and ones that you don't.

The table above generates a brief understanding of what traits are desirable in recognition with particular job positions. You must take into consideration, that while you might not possess all the characteristics that employers are looking for, it will give you some understanding whether you are a strong enough candidate to apply for that particular job position.

TRAITS USUALLY GO TOGETHER

Personality tests are used to gain insight and understanding into an individual's personality. A person's personality tells employers a great deal about whether or not they are right for the job. Employers look for particular personality traits regarding the job position that is being applied for and so demonstrating that a person has those traits is important.

Personality traits reflect how a person is perceived. They are able to distinguish their abilities and strengths in order to assess their level of success rate. Traits often indicate other important traits. For example, if a person is considered artistic, it means that this person will also be considered as creative.

Below is a table that indicates some common personality traits and the traits which are often associated with them.

TRAITS	TRAITS THAT ARE COMMONLY ASSOCIATED
Creative	Artistic, critical thinker, ambitious, flexible, motivated
Perseverance	Ambitious, motivated, self-disciplined, compliant, reliable, gritted, conscientious
Adaptable	Self-disciplined, reliable, flexible
Conscientious	Aware, thorough, careful, vigilant, organised, dependable
Optimistic	Content, positive, enthusiastic
Resilient	Aware, controlled, strong-minded, adverse
Sales and negotiation	Dominant, compliant, straightforward, warmth, social comfort
Dynamic	Eager, active, resilient, open, independent, confident
Assertive	Confident, assured, competent, expressive, self-assured, affirmative
Tolerant	Resistant, dominant, self-disciplined, aware, broad-minded
Competent	Skilled, knowledgeable, dominant, independent
Vulnerable	Self-conscious, pessimistic, anxious, immature, inexperienced
Trusting	Team player, social comfort, open, gregarious, altruistic, unassuming
Ambitious	Goal orientated, achievement striving, confident, capable, active, outgoing, motivated
Daydreamer	Immature, vulnerable, unrealistic
Critical thinking	Disciplined, dominant, self-sufficient, independent, experienced, competent

TRAITS	TRAITS THAT ARE COMMONLY ASSOCIATED
Independent	Capable, self-sufficient, logical, flexible, assertive
Self-disciplined	Independent, dutiful, positive, persistent, productive
Social comfort	Confident, gregarious, positive, active, team player
Competitive	Achievement striving, self-disciplined, motivated, ambitious, dominant, vigilant
Direct	Affirmative, dominant, perseverance, thorough, confident
Empathetic	Team player, sympathetic, social comfort
Active	Persistent, dynamic, dominant, self-assured, motivated
Dutiful	Obedient, reliable, self-sufficient, motivated, self-disciplined, deliberated
Team player	Social comfort, trusting, compliant, order, dutiful

It is important to understand that these personality tests used in the recruitment and selection process are the basis to identify personality that employers want. Employers use these tests to pinpoint strong candidates and determine a candidate's personality.

The table above indicates some of the main personality traits that are often analysed or referred to and how this relates to other traits.

This test is not designed to give you a definite answer. It is merely a way of exploring your personality and gain an understanding of the type of personality that you have. It allows you to answer lots of sample questions and work out what personality traits you have and how this is perceived in your chosen career.

This test is designed so that you are given an insight into what different job roles look for in terms of personality and how it is explored.

Hopefully, from working through this book, you have been able to identify your key strengths and some undesirable qualities which you can use to work on in regards to achieving your career goals. Remember, it takes a matter of seconds to make an impression on someone, so you want to be assured that you come across as the type of person who is right for the job role.

Do your research! Focus on what employers are looking for and apply yourself to the requirements which they give. If they do present you with a personality test, you will now be ready to answer it not only with honesty, but with knowledge of what to expect.

Good luck in all your future job endeavours!

Get more books, manuals, online tests and training courses at:

www.How2Become.com